7 Secrets of Time Travel

"Thanks to the clarity of his insights and the freshness of his perspective, Von Braschler's guide to time travel is our handbook to new, unchartered realms of experience and healing. The vehicle he offers is not a relatively crude 'machine' but the sublime human soul. In short, he tells us that we do not have to wait for the invention of some promised technology. On the contrary, we have been carrying around within us, since the day we were born, everything we need for visiting the past or future. He lays out seven secrets to access this wonderful mystery, clearly and convincingly describing them as the cornerstones of his practical guide."

FRANK JOSEPH, AUTHOR OF *ATLANTIS AND 2012*
AND *GODS OF THE RUNES*

7 Secrets of Time Travel

Mystic Voyages *of the* Energy Body

VON BRASCHLER

Destiny Books
Rochester, Vermont • Toronto, Canada

Destiny Books
One Park Street
Rochester, Vermont 05767
www.DestinyBooks.com

Text stock is SFI certified

Destiny Books is a division of Inner Traditions International

Library of Congress Cataloging-in-Publication Data
Braschler, Von, 1947–
  Seven secrets of time travel : mystic voyages of the energy body / Von Braschler.
    p. cm.
  Summary: "How to break free from the physical world and travel via the energy
body"—Provided by publisher.
  Includes bibliographical references (p.   ) and index.
  ISBN 978-1-59477-447-8 (pbk.) — ISBN 978-1-59477-695-3 (e-book)
  1. Spiritual healing. 2. Time travel. 3. Astral projection. 4. Seven rays
(Occultism) I. Title.
  BF1999.B6673 2012
  133.9'5—dc23
                                                                2011045075

Printed and bound in the United States by Lake Book Manufacturing
The text stock is SFI certified. The Sustainable Forestry Initiative® program
promotes sustainable forest management.

10   9   8   7   6   5   4   3   2   1

Text design by Priscilla H. Baker
Text layout by Virginia Scott Bowman
This book was typeset in Garamond Premier Pro and Gill Sans with Helios and
Helvetica Neue used as display typefaces

To send correspondence to the author of this book, mail a first-class letter to the
author c/o Inner Traditions • Bear & Company, One Park Street, Rochester, VT
05767, and we will forward the communication.

Dedicated to the
Physicians Committee for Responsible Medicine

Traveling freely beyond frozen time,
where real change becomes possible!

Contents

Foreword

Since the publication of H. G. Wells's *The Time Machine* in 1895, generations have dreamed of traveling backward into the past or forward into the future. What was once popular fantasy, however, is now becoming scientific speculation as cosmologists and physicists debate possibilities for traversing the temporal boundaries of our present world. Breaking the time limit is said to lie within the potential of technology. But this view is unchanged from Wells's Victorian-era mentality, which envisioned materialistic science as humankind's salvation and inevitable godhood. Unfortunately, the development of advanced weaponry in the centuries after the release of his novel tragically dashed this naive hope.

Von Braschler focuses instead on a metaphysical means of applied time travel. The expedient is not something outside ourselves but within us. The vehicle he offers is not a relatively crude "machine" but the sublime human soul. In short, he tells us that we do not have to wait for the invention of some promised technology. On the contrary, we have been carrying around within us, since the day we were born, everything we need for visiting the past or future.

Von Braschler lays out seven secrets to access this wonderful mystery, clearly and convincingly describing them as the cornerstones of his practical guide to time travel. He does not trivialize the subject, however, nor mislead readers by making promises he cannot keep. His emphasis is instead on true healing—in the higher, spiritual sense of wholeness—in the context of the Eternal Now, in a moment beyond time.

I am not entirely unfamiliar with these ideas, because Von Braschler has shared some of them with me during the course of our friendship over the years. It has been my honor and pleasure to know him since 1991, when, as a promotions director at Llewellyn Publications in St. Paul, Minnesota, he played a critical role in the success of my first book, *Sacred Sites: A Guidebook to Mysterious Places*. More than twenty books later, I have come to admire him as much for the integrity of his soul as for the impressive scope of his intellect. These superlative qualities shine throughout the pages of Von's latest book, which seems destined to become a true classic of its kind. In any case, it is sure to ignite new interest in a subject already experiencing growing controversy around the world.

Thanks to the clarity of his insights and the freshness of his perspective, Von Braschler's practical guide to time travel is our handbook to new, uncharted realms of experience and healing.

FRANK JOSEPH

Frank Joseph is the editor in chief of *Ancient American* magazine and the author of *Advanced Civilizations of Prehistoric America, Atlantis and 2012, The Destruction of Atlantis, Gods of the Runes, The Lost Civilization of Lemuria, The Lost Treasure of King Juba*, and *Survivors of Atlantis*.

SEVEN SECRETS OF TIME, TIMELESSNESS, AND TIME TRAVEL

1. Time, as we know it, is simply an illusion of this earth plane with physical limitations.

2. There is personal power in the present moment.

3. Time = Energy = Opportunity = Karma

4. Timelessness is just beyond time as we know it.

5. You can traverse time and merge time lines.

6. You can heal and effect real change outside space and time.

7. The primal power of the seven rays defines our opportunities.

Introduction

This new book that you hold in your hands is the evolution of *Perfect Timing* and *Chakra Reading & Color Healing,* my earlier books that outline healing exercises that I have practiced with workshop and lecture groups throughout the country and even on television and the radio. What has evolved is my own understanding of time, aided by my study of ancient mystics, modern healers, and cutting-edge nuclear physicists.

Those earlier ventures into various states of consciousness and creative visualization were based on the popular notion that all of the power for change is locked in the present moment or what Eastern philosophies call the Eternal Now. Certainly, the present moment is the point in time where individuals who hope to concentrate their full attention in meditation must learn to focus. When we focus solely on the present moment, we turn off the endless mind loop of chatter within us that diverts our attention to worries about the future and regrets about the past. That enables us to reach a quiet stillness deep within us where spirit resides. Spirit is our energy life force, that invisible side of us that often takes a back seat to all of the sensations and cravings of the physical body. When we awaken the spirit within us by stilling the mind and numbing the physical body for only a few moments, it puts us in synch with the eternal life force that permeates all of creation.

What I discovered in leading healing meditations and consciousness exercises with workshop groups at the prestigious Omega Institute of Holistic Studies and other locations around the country is that entering the Eternal Now and the power of the present moment only opens the door to change. Healing "takes time," as the saying goes. "Time heals old wounds," we are told. Medical people often tell us that "it's going to take just a little time" to see improvement. Certainly, we tend to measure time by change. In our commitment to personal change in our lives, we are willing to take time. We become devoted to this all-important time that seems necessary to our healing. We feel that we have to "put in the time." So we patiently wait.

We all seek to *change* our present condition because we suffer. We suffer in different ways, of course, but we all suffer. The Buddha explained that suffering was the universal human condition, due to our lack of understanding. Sometimes our hurt is not even obvious, but is hidden within the many layers of our being. Other times, what ails us becomes grossly obvious to the eye as it eats away at our physical body. For many people, the ailment is emotional, mental, or spiritual, but what bothers us on emotional, mental, and spiritual levels can impact us ultimately on the physical level.

Western medical science now basically agrees with ancient Eastern views on human makeup in admitting the complexity of our being. The Indian Hindu view sees the physical body with subtle energy layers that account for our emotional being, mental being, causal being, and spiritual connectedness to everything. Modern Western medical people now acknowledge that how things affect us on a spiritual, mental, or emotional level can descend into physical symptoms that are real enough to cause us pain and disabilities. So they seek to treat the whole patient—body, mind, and soul.

Recovery means different things to different people. It can mean breaking a pattern of addiction, psychological healing, or overcoming personal problems that are buried deep in our souls. Everybody, however, wants to heal. Everybody wants to become a healthier person, free from pain and stress.

Real healing must seem practically impossible to most people. They look for someone to heal them, thinking that they cannot heal themselves. Almost everyone in the medical community and the healing arts, on the other hand, recognizes that true healing happens from the inside, with the sick healing themselves. So-called healers only assist in this natural process. The human body can be self-rejuvenating. It is a self-correcting dynamo in many regards. Patients can only recover if they want to and if they focus their will on this natural process of self-regeneration. Nobody can take the pills for us when we are sick. Nobody can exercise our body during our rehabilitation. Others can only assist us.

The human body is a miraculous creation. Our broken bones tend to heal. The body's immune system, if operating correctly, fights for our recovery. But there are limitations in a physical world that is fixed in time and space. What doesn't freely enter the physical world of fixed time and space is pure energy, which we need to reenergize ourselves. Pure energy lives outside space and time, from where it transforms into latent material forms in the physical world. We can think of energy as the great void from which all things come, a world of limitless possibilities that exist in an unmanifest state. In the great void of unmanifested energy, time does not occur in the sense that we have concocted as a convenient measurement with our clocks and calendars. Things occur in their own sense of time and are measured more by duration than by any arbitrary measuring stick that linear thinkers might devise.

People, after all, live relatively brief lives in the grand scheme of creation, so we attempt to establish some comfortable sense of continuity by showing events in endless motion with clocklike regularity. We combine a lot of frozen images that our eyes snap up like a camera and play them inside our little brains like a motion picture. Perhaps that makes us feel that life endures with smooth, recognizable continuity.

In truth, time, as we generally perceive it, does not exist. There is, of course, solar time. Everything else is a creative myth that we have all agreed to accept. If we really think about it, we must recognize that not every second, minute, or hour is the same as we experience it. Sometimes an hour seems to pass very slowly. At other times, an hour disappears quickly in our experience. What varies is our perception.

We live in a frozen world where energy has manifested itself in a material form. As physical creatures in a physical world, we tend to think only of material existence and try to resolve everything in this solid, fixed state. So we heat things up and change chemical compositions in the false belief that we can escape the physical limitations of the material world and really change things. But turning a solid into a liquid does not make it less physical, nor does changing a liquid into a gas. Nothing we do physically will allow us to escape the laws of physics and our fixed place in space and time.

The world of Now is where we live physically. On this physical level of existence, what we perceive as creation is frozen in time. A great idea for a dynamic play becomes words frozen on a page. A musical composition becomes frozen in time as notes on sheets of paper or physical recordings that never change. The most fluid and dynamic painting becomes locked in time at the moment the brush strokes of the master dry on the canvas. The creative architect's dream of a building that is intended to blend with its natural surroundings becomes frozen form as brick and glass. Every creation that people like us ever imagined and then executed became frozen in space and time at the moment it was physically constructed. The great pyramids have stood for thousands and thousands of years, changing very little before our eyes, as erosion occurs outside of our perceived time line over a long, uncertain duration.

My practice of leading exercises in meditative healing based on time awareness taught me that we cannot alter physical form in the frozen world of material existence. I realized that real change is made possible by using meditation as a doorway to enter timelessness outside of physical space and time, where energy can be moved by spirit. I also determined with our diverse class at Omega Institute and at other settings like Transitions in Chicago and Angels Forever/Windows of Light in

Wisconsin that anyone can learn to enter a meditative state quite easily. Most people who meditate, however, have a limited view of what meditation can accomplish. The goal of the highest form of meditation is not quiet reflection, inner reflection, or simply sensory deprivation to enter a different brain wave pattern. Rather, the goal is to enter a state of heightened consciousness without physical distraction, with a shift from sensory perception to awareness in a spirit body. That spirit body, with its own perceptive awareness, can operate outside of the physical body as pure consciousness outside of physical space and time.

This is the unseen world that your physical body often refuses to recognize for fear of lack of control. But when your physical body is safely tucked away in a quiet, secluded setting during controlled meditation, the spirit inside you—your body double—can freely leave the limitations of physical form. Your spirit longs to be free and soar outside of the restrictive laws of physics that have no real hold on it, to enter timelessness, where pure energy exists and meaningful change is possible.

P. D. Ouspensky, early Theosophist and biographer of the mystic G. I. Gurdjieff, wrote in his classic *Tertium Organum* that we can use meditation to reach heightened consciousness and awareness and escape the limited dimensions of our physical world. Our spirit can soar beyond our fixed location on this plane of existence. Beyond this plane we can find everything else in all of creation—universes layered atop other universes and realities layered atop our limited mundane reality.

The exercises in this new book show ways to escape the limitations of physical time and space to enter a world of pure energy and spirit where change is readily possible. So in a real sense, this is a book about healing and time travel. Our exercises might seem to take you back in time or even forward in time. Keep in mind, however, that time—or what we commonly consider time—is actually flexible and fluid. It can bend back on itself. The past and future can exist simultaneously, depending on our ability or conscious awareness to perceive them. If we can look into the past or the future, then time is not linear at all. It is transmutable, to use a term from mystical alchemy. And as we learn to

move freely through timelessness in an energy body of pure consciousness, we become agents of change.

Time might be an illusion, but change is not. The role of people
as part of the human process of living is to bring about change. That's
what living in this earthly existence is all about: making a difference,
transformation. Much of the change we dream about and work to
achieve, however, is difficult because of the limitations in the natural
laws of physics that restrict us. It is difficult to bring energy into our
lives because we live in the world of matter, which is the manifestation
of energy in a fixed or frozen form. We have made things even more
difficult for ourselves by living apart from nature and apart from spirit,
two things akin to energy.

It is my sincere desire that you find the time-shift exercises and
healing meditations in this guidebook helpful in bringing you closer to
the natural spirit world of pure energy where real change is possible. I
hope that you will experience this sort of real change on a personal level
in a way that will transform your life.

First Secret of Time

TIME IS AN ILLUSION OF THIS EARTH PLANE WITH PHYSICAL LIMITATIONS

To many people, time remains the most fascinating and mystical subject on earth. We never seem to have enough time, yet on occasion it seems to drag by too slowly, regardless of our feeble efforts to control it. Despite our efforts to create exacting timepieces, count fractions of a second, and organize our lives with orderly time zones and daylight savings time, we do not appear any closer to mastering time. To the contrary, time seems to have mastered us. We try to stretch or condense time to get more out of each day. Many people keep one eye on their watch throughout the day and become nervous wrecks for all of their diligent clock watching.

I'm certain that you have personally experienced how much longer it seems to take water to boil when you are watching it impatiently. At other times, it boils over before you are ready for it. And you have probably noticed how quickly a good party or holiday passes by, while dreary, agonizing encounters seem to drag on at a snail's pace. Despite our inability to control time, we seem convinced that modern technology will give us some mastery over it. We appear somewhat like speedy little flying bugs caught in a web, cocky that our ability to bounce up and down and side to side will set us free.

The human obsession with controlling time seems particularly true of modern society. We have gone from classic sundials to hourglasses, clocks, wristwatches, and now digital and atomic timepieces. However, this escalation in our attempts to measure time has not given us any more control over it. Most of us find too little daylight at the end of a busy day and too little nighttime for the sleep we deny ourselves in a quest to cram more action into a finite number of hours each hectic day. Many people keep little day planners with them at all times so that they don't waste a single, precious moment by not being conscious of time escaping from them. We are so very worried about losing time and letting minutes slip away from us.

Our ancient ancestors assumed a very different approach to dealing with time. They rose in the morning when the sun lighted up their faces. They paced themselves throughout the early, soft light of morning, filled with all of the possibilities for those who rise early. They recognized midday and the long afternoon when the sun completed its descending arc on the planet, a time of greater warmth when activities of the day could be settled or put to rest. When the sun would set, many activities of the day would end. It was a quiet time for the family meal, discussion, or reflection on events of the day and plans for tomorrow. As the world fell into darkness, our ancestors used that opportunity for needed rest. Apparently our ancestors had fewer problems from sleep deprivation than we busy moderns who try to burn the candle at both ends. Today, we want to get more out of each day, and we look for ways to escape the limitations of time.

We are fascinated by the possibility of time travel or time machines that might allow us free movement outside the confines of the frozen moments at hand. We seem desperate to escape the present moment and be somewhere else, thinking perhaps that the future will be more promising or the past more comfortable. Many people, feeling the sting of modern problems, might long for a time when life seemed more leisurely and relaxed, without the stress of modern life. Indeed, our labor-saving devices, intended to free up blocks of leisure time, appear instead to have enslaved us. Now we must find extra time for our computer, our cell phone, our dishwasher, our robot vacuum, and numerous appointments with service providers from garages, government agencies, clinics, and hair salons, all of whom attempt to schedule us and manage us in an orderly matrix of appointment charts that are maintained within fifteen-minute increments. Behind all of this is the human urge to manage our destiny and take control of our day-to-day events so that we feel in control of our world and that we are moving forward progressively. We want to feel that we are advancing from point A to point B efficiently and not just standing still or going in circles.

Being able to measure everything gives us the illusion that we have control over it. So we hold measuring sticks against everything that we see. Once we have catalogued everything, we can put things into little compartments in our mind with a sense of control. We want everything to be measurable and orderly. As linear thinkers in a physical world, we want to think of everything in such simplistic terms. We want to reach that finish line in record time; that makes us feel like winners. Not moving forward through time makes us feel like losers. Our dreams of a time machine that can be driven like a vehicle down a straight road represent our very human hope that we can move from point A to point B in an orderly fashion, whether we are going forward or backward.

But, as Marshall McLuhan argued, our linear thinking is short-sighted. We become pretty much lost in trying to understand what lies behind a flat-world, two-dimensional approach to our environment. What if time isn't like a ribbon that we lay out from a starting point to a finish line? What if time is really flexible? What if that neat, straight ribbon of time in our mind is really a twisted ribbon that curls and loops around and back on itself in a way that has no recognizable starting point or end line?

TWO VIEWS OF TIME

People have long been mystified by time. Philosophers and scientists over the past 2,500 years have attempted to put it into proper perspective. Aristotle, Leibniz, Newton, Kant, and everyone before Einstein seemed to suggest a frame-independent duration between events. According to German rational philosopher and mathematician Gottfried Wilhelm Leibniz (1646–1716), time does not really exist, but is the conceptual order that our minds place on existence. Leibniz took a spiritual approach to his description of time. He saw the universe as containing only God and noncomposite, immaterial, soul-like entities called "monads." He believed that time, space, cause, and matter, as we normally conceive of them, are simply illusions. These illusions are well founded, however, and explained by the true nature of our universe at its fundamental level.

The eighteenth-century Prussian philosopher Immanuel Kant wrote that time and space are forms that the human mind projects on things external. He theorized that the mind structures perception so that time follows a mathematical line and conforms to Euclidean geometry. He suggested that people have no direct perception of time, but only an ability to experience things and events in time. Hence, time is a convenience to keep our thoughts about the world orderly.

Kant suggested a subtle relationship between time and the mind. He believed that our mind actually structures our perceptions in a way that we know a priori, instinctively. Time for Kant was dependent on personal conscious experience. We cannot overlook the obvious role of individual perception in personal observation of how time plays out for each one of us. Sometimes, under certain circumstances, we might perceive time as passing slowly, while other times the perception is that it seems to fly by quickly.

Albert Einstein's special theory of relativity modified Kant's space + time vision to include the notion of space-time. In this theory, space-time can be intersected by a *now* plane in different ways with different angles, so that our sense of things occurring simultaneously is dependent on the state of motion. Einstein declared that the time interval between two events depends on the observer's reference frame. "Every reference-body," he wrote, "has its own particular time; unless we are told the reference-body to which the statement of time refers, there is no meaning in a statement of the time of an event." Consequently, Einstein viewed each reference frame or reference body as dividing space-time differently into its time part and its space part.

All of physics to date, however, including quantum mechanics, has been based on the space + time vision of time as phrased by Aristotle, Newton, Kant, and even Einstein. British physicist Julian Barbour's departure from traditional views on time in his groundbreaking book *The End of Time* suggests a total reconstruction of physics in a way that would probably have pleased Leibniz. This celebrated book stunned the world with the pronouncement that there is no real change in our world and that all the change and motion that we perceive is illusion, which exists only in our mind. With Barbour, we see a modern nuclear physicist agreeing with a seventeenth-century rational philosopher that change doesn't really exist, as we perceive it, and neither does time.

Barbour argues that there is only solar time in our physical world here on earth. The sun rises at a certain time, depending on where we live on our world. It advances across the land throughout the solar day. The sun affects our weather and how our lives go, according to conditions it creates on the land. The magnetic pull of the moon, as a reflection of the sun, affects the tides of the vast waters that cover our world. The solar day is what governs all life on earth. Beyond that, time is pretty much a human invention or an abstraction at which we arrive by means of the changes in things, as renowned Austrian physicist Ernest Mach once said.

TIME = CHANGE

For Barbour, the only way we seem to experience time at all is through snapshots that record our memory of an event at any one point. What we experience, he said is an *instant*. People tend to think of time as endlessly flowing forward, but that's not how we experience it. Barbour points out that almost everyone seems to see time as something linear, as a series of individual instants strung on an endless line. So Barbour sees people experiencing time like passengers on a train, imagining that they are progressing through time. They seem to be moving forward. But are they really? Every stop on the train is a new instant. The Now is ever changing.

Even the way we seem to conceptualize the flow of events in a dance performance is contrived, based actually on independent snapshots or moments that we have recorded and chosen to play in our brain as continuous time in motion. We see and record the position of the dancer as proceeding instants. Our brain, however, can't process data instantaneously. So we encode several independent images of the performance. The brain, Barbour says, interprets the collection of snapshots it has encoded as it plays them for us as a motion picture. He asks whether the image is really moving, or are we simply moving a collection of still pictures to create the illusion of time and motion in our mind?

We invented the motion picture to give us the impression that our many present moments could be fast-forwarded in a blur of pictures that resemble continuous movement and continuation through time. In truth, this is an illusion. Part of entering and accepting the fantasy of a motion picture seems to involve suspending critical thought and just believing what you see or think you see. That's true even of simple instructional films. I remember one of my first jobs in college was to run films for the nursing classes. Obviously, this predated DVD projectors. I didn't really know how to run a movie projector when I took this little part-time job, but figured that it couldn't be hard. I'd seen lots of movies. I figured that somebody just flipped a switch and the movie reel turned around and around. Well, the film broke on my first day, when I tried to loop it and feed it into the projector. When I looked at the broken film, I realized for the first time that it was really a series of still frames strung together to create the effect of watching events in motion. In frame 1, the actor is standing. Then in frame 2, the actor begins to extend one leg in a walking motion. In frame 3, the leg is extended a little farther in this walking motion. In fact, the moving picture evolved from the old flip-books that people used to assemble like a deck of cards. Each page showed a different scene. The many scenes depicted on the pages of the book would appear to have motion when the pages were flipped rapidly.

When I accidentally broke the film loop into two strands it made the optical trick of mass deception of a movie rather obvious. It's not much different with DVD disks that hold movies. The disks contain a series of individual sectors or segments that play in succession with the aid of a DVD player that rotates the disk. This is the same way we sequence the snapshots that our eyes as human cameras record. We arrange a series of related snapshots in a sequence to give us the sense of motion going forward. Perhaps our attempts to sense progressive continuity come from a human desire to outlive our physical death.

MERGING PHYSICS AND METAPHYSICS

Barbour says that time and change are connected. According to this view we might even say that time measures change. When something fundamentally changes in a transformative way, then time has elapsed (although it might be better to say that its time has come).

Such a scientific description of time as dependent on change is consistent with the mystical distinction outlined by H. P. Blavatsky in her groundbreaking book *The Secret Doctrine,* cribbed from what she described as a most ancient document protected by Tibetan masters in the Himalayas. Blavatsky is known today as the truth seeker who brought to the West the esoteric wisdom traditions of the East. A bold explorer, she found her own way up the Himalayan mountains to a hidden spiritual retreat where adept masters of various origins and traditions had maintained the esoteric truths handed down from the beginning of our history to those few who sought the truth and could understand it. With the help of these masters, who acted as her teachers and guides, she read, memorized, and transcribed the ancient texts.

In *The Secret Doctrine,* Madame Blavatsky considers how creation is measured chronologically, not in terms of time as we commonly measure things, but in terms of how long *change* takes to occur. This is a somewhat practical description, acknowledging a passage of time that can be measured by obvious change. She uses the term *duration* to measure how long significant change requires, suggesting that we must shift our view of time to vast arcs of transformation, as seen in glacial ages, eons, and epochs. Change takes however long it must take in order for transformation to occur. Nature does not reckon time the way we commonly measure it in seconds and minutes. How long does it take a glacier to form and melt? How long does rock take to erode and dissolve into sand?

Blavatsky, as a cofounder of the Theosophical Society, sought to merge scientific discovery with the occult view of creation in a wisdom tradition as old as Plato or older. She felt that science would eventually catch up with the esoteric worldview and reconcile itself with the mystic's view of creation, both in terms of cosmogenesis and anthropogenesis. We see in nuclear physics and holistic science today the fulfillment of her vision back in the late nineteenth century.

Blavatsky and her fellow Theosophists, in fact, encouraged the merged study of science, religion, and philosophy as equally important and related disciplines and declared this three-pronged approach to open-minded study one of the major objectives for the Theosophical Society. This approach—with its lack of dogma, emphasis on individual freedom of interpretation, and motto "There is no religion higher than truth"—attracted some of the greatest minds of the time. A short list includes Sir Arthur Conan Doyle, Piet Mondrian, P. D. Ouspensky, Rudolph Steiner, Maria Montessori, Jiddu Krishnamurti, Albert Einstein, Thomas Edison, Abner Doubleday, and Frank Bohm, author of the Wizard of Oz series of books.

She also wrote about the role of the observer with regard to relativity, before Einstein's now-famous theories of relativity put the observer squarely in the middle of things. She said in *The Secret Doctrine* that everything that exists has only a relative and not an absolute reality, since the appearance that the hidden *noumenon* (intellectual conception) assumes for an observer depends on that observer's power of cognition. All things, then, are relatively real, as the observer is also a reflection and the things being observed are real to the observer.

Curiously, Einstein thoroughly read Madame Blavatsky's contemporary *Secret Doctrine* and its ancient, mystical descriptions of cosmology and the nature of reality. He left his dog-eared first-edition copy with numerous marginal notes and underlining for his niece to discover by his side when he died. He'd obviously read it very carefully, and probably many times, judging from its wear. (She later hand-carried his copy of the book to the Theosophical Society to place in the library. It now resides in the library at Adyar, India, the society's international headquarters.)

In her book, Blavatsky also suggests that energy in the form of electricity, electromagnetism, light, and heat represents a supersensuous state of matter in motion and that all of these forces of nature are differentiated aspects of the universal motion of the universe. This is interestingly in accord with the laws of conservation of mass and thermodynamics, which grew out of the work of two scientists of the eighteenth century.

One of them, French tax collector Antoine Lavoisier, is known as the father of chemistry. Lavoisier's book *Elementary Treatise of Chemistry* (1789) was the first modern chemical textbook, which presented a united view of new theories of chemistry. He also proved the law of conservation of mass, which holds that matter is neither created nor destroyed. He showed that the mass of substances or reactants in a closed system will remain constant, regardless of what processes are acting inside the system. Matter might change form, but the mass of the reactants must always equal the mass of the products. If burning sulfur increases its weight, then something (air) has been added to it.

When Lavoisier started his experiments on combustion and respiration, chemistry was still in the earliest stages of development. Lavoisier, who later lost his head on the guillotine in the French Revolution, spent a personal fortune on scientific instruments to create modern chemistry. This included precise measuring instruments to determine the weight gain of material matter. In order to make such careful measurements, he invented a balance that was good to approximately 0.0005 gram. In precise experiments, he showed that *matter does not change* significantly without adding to it or deleting from it. Even today, this discovery seems startling to many, who view the physical world as filled with abundant potential for change on a material level.

Earlier than Lavoisier's experiments, Mikhail Lomonosov had expressed similar ideas in 1748. Hence, the law of conservation of mass (or matter) is also widely known as the Lomonosov-Lavoisier law, since Lavoisier proved the earlier theory of Lomonosov.

In modern physics, the principle of conservation of mass for closed systems continues to hold true. This means that in most situations the law of conservation of mass can be assumed valid, except that it is harder to prove true when speeds approach the speed of light, at which point mass begins transforming into energy. Consequently, we now have the law of conservation of mass and energy. The law of matter conservation can be considered an approximate physical law that holds in the classical sense, from before the advent of special relativity and quantum mechanics.

The Lomonosov-Lavoisier law is the central idea behind the first law of thermodynamics. Thermodynamics is the study of energy. Energy exists in many forms, such as heat, light, chemical energy, and electrical energy. Energy is the ability to bring about change.

The first law of thermodynamics states that energy is always conserved and cannot be created or destroyed. In essence, energy can be converted from one form into another. The total amount of energy and matter in the known universe remains constant.

The second law of thermodynamics states that in all energy

exchanges, the potential energy of the state will always be less than that of the initial state, if no energy enters or leaves the system. This is commonly called *entropy*. The flow of energy maintains life. Entropy wins whenever organisms cease to take in energy and die.

ELECTROMAGNETIC ENERGY FIELDS

In her occult classic Blavatsky describes an unknowable, unfathomable, and mysterious ultimate reality behind all of life. She says that we can never fully understand or comprehend this absolute reality, but that it permeates and inhabits all of creation above and below, from rock to tree and animal, in a way that makes all of life interdependent and interrelated. We are all made of star stuff and energized from the same source. This is what other mystics have called *Spirit* or *Akasha*. From it, all nature proceeds. Into it, all life returns at the end of life cycles.

Furthermore, her ascetic teachers, the Mahatmas or Himalayan brotherhood, taught her the ancient mystery of *fohat* as a universal propelling vital force. In nature, it is the essence of cosmic electricity. In the manifest universe, it is the ever-present electrical energy and ceaseless destructive and formative power. Perhaps this is what our cutting-edge scientists now call electromagnetism and the electromagnetic field.

Electromagnetic fields are present everywhere on the earth and in space. They undergo wave motion, which spreads with the speed of light. We know that they are produced in the molten core of the earth, the rarefied gas of space, and the glowing heat of sunspots, but finding out how they are produced remains somewhat of a challenge to us. Solar electromagnetic energy powers our world. In the form of light, it produces photosynthesis to make our world green and growing with abundant plant life. The electromagnetic field that surrounds and inhabits our physical bodies energizes us and empowers us. We might add that human consciousness and thought-forms are electromagnetic energy dispatched in wave motion.

Blavatsky's partner and cofounder of the Theosophical Society was

Col. Henry Steele Olcott, who had served in the U.S. Civil War and headed the investigation into the conspiracy to assassinate President Abraham Lincoln. He also had an inquiring mind and was an author in the area of metaphysics and esoteric matters. Originally trained as a lawyer and journalist, he became fascinated by the experiments conducted in the 1770s by German physician Franz Anton Mesmer. Today we often think of Mesmer in regard to his contribution to hypnotism and the term *mesmerize*. Mesmer's experiments sought to display the power of electromagnetism, which he saw as a cure for many ailments. He tested his theory in controversial public displays. In one experiment he charged or "mesmerized" a tub of water with his own magnetic energy. This has been replicated by the scientific researcher and physician Andrija Puharich, who observed psychic Uri Geller charge a glass of water with his hands. The point was the same. Electromagnetic energy from the human body can charge water with healing properties.

This is something I have personally experienced. I have written elsewhere about how I was given a glass of water that had been personally magnetized by the human hand of a healer and electromagnetically charged with a quartz crystal with its piezoelectric properties. The result was smooth, sweet water that made me feel better almost instantly.

Col. Olcott was fascinated by the way Mesmer had charged a tub of water with electromagnetic energy for healing. He wrote extensively in various essays in the periodical *The Theosophist* and his published memoirs, *Old Diary Leaves,* about his belief in electricity and magnetism as physical manifestations of a great, primal force in nature. (Indeed, physics now treats electromagnetism as one of the four fundamental forces in nature, the others being gravity, weak interaction, and strong interaction. All other forces in nature spring from these four primary forces.)

Olcott saw that the power of electricity and magnetism was within our grasp to harness naturally, and he set about healing people with the energy in his hands. He visited Ceylon (now Sri Lanka) at the end of the nineteenth century and did two things for the people there. He introduced them to Buddhism and healed the sick. Now, many energy healers claim to heal somebody from time to time, and our medical community often considers their success rate exaggerated. Col. Olcott, however, healed thousands of people in old Ceylon with the electromagnetic energy of his hands. He is revered in that ancient land for his tangible contributions there.

To say that Olcott healed by controlling the energy waves within his own electromagnetic field, however, is an incomplete explanation. Like most Theosophists of his time and since, Olcott believed in thought power and the concept that our consciousness can energize the intent and power of our will. This Theosophical view, based on the ageless wisdom that Blavatsky brought down from the hidden Himalayan retreat of the adepts, holds that our thoughts can assume form and be directed like energy waves from our consciousness outward. Or, to be more precise, our consciousness can be directed precisely like energy waves. Part of the cosmological model that Blavatsky found in the adepts' hidden mountain retreat was *as above, so below.* This view is part of an Eastern philosophy that suggests our bodies mirror the greater cosmos in microcosm. The new electromagnetic energy field theory seems to agree with that holistic view.

Electromagnetic fields everywhere describe electromagnetic interaction. The field is the combination of an electric field produced by stationary charges and a magnetic field produced by moving charges or currents. Traditionally scientists believed that electric and magnetic fields were produced by smooth motions of charged objects. Oscillating charges, for example, produce electrical and magnetic fields that can be seen in a continuous, wave-like pattern. In such cases, energy is seen as being transferred continuously through an electromagnetic field between any two locations. The electromagnetic field, however, can be viewed in a more coarse way. It has been shown that electromagnetic energy transfer is best described as being carried in bits called photons with a fixed frequency. The quantum view of electromagnetic fields has successfully led to quantum electrodynamics, a field theory that describes the interaction of electromagnetic radiation with charged matter.

Once an electromagnetic field is produced from a given charge distribution, other charged objects in this field will experience a force similar to that felt by planets in experiencing the gravitational force of the sun. If these other charges and currents are comparable in size to the source of the electromagnetic field, then a new electromagnetic field will be produced. Consequently, an electromagnetic field can be considered a *dynamic* entity that causes other charges and currents to move and is also affected by them.

Our thoughts and emotions also can be viewed as energy and part of the human electromagnetic field. The electrical charges that course through our brains can be measured on electroencephalograms. Stimuli pass through sensory memory and are carried by the nervous system to the brain. The energy of human thought waves has been shown to change the structure of matter, as demonstrated in Masaru Emoto's *The Hidden Messages in Water*. Positive thoughts in meditation, vocalization, or even written thoughts can alter water, changing its basic pH level and giving it crystalline structure. Music also has been shown to have an effect on water, changing it substantially. Even prior to the publication of his book, Emoto's experiments, which measure the human ability to alter water with thoughts and personal touch, had already been replicated throughout the world. Since the publication of the book, even more researchers have successfully replicated his experiments in the power of human consciousness.

MEASURING HUMAN ENERGY FIELDS

Human consciousness as an energy field that we can direct for change has been described by Harvard Medical School's David McClelland, Ph.D. He described what he calls the "Mother Teresa effect," whereby people effectively send thoughts of love to heal the sick. In similar research, American physicist Jack Sarfatti has demonstrated that consciousness is composed of tiny resonating strings that create an electromagnetic energy field that resonates at a particular frequency. Sarfatti showed how this can be mathematically quantified. Energy directed in the manner of McClelland's "love thoughts" or Emoto's "thought-forms" has both a transmitter and receiver.

I have personally observed and measured electromagnetic energy being directed from the human body. Years ago, I built a Kirlian camera. It was a smaller version of the famous device used to measure human bioelectric plasma, which was developed in Russia in the 1930s by scientists Semyon and Valentina Kirlian. My smaller Kirlian camera worked much the same as the original device. It sandwiched a subject between two electrode plates. Normally this would be something like a person's fingertip. Then when an electrical stimulation is applied, a corona discharge seems to take place between the subject and the plates. One explanation for this result is that this discharge is the result of molecules that ionize and form small lightning bolts from the object through the film to the electrode plates.

The experiments of the Kirlians, disclosed in the book *Psychic Discoveries behind the Iron Curtain,* proved hard to replicate in the West. However, over the years I have successfully done so. To me, the little Kirlian camera I built seemed to capture light in a bottle. It was like no other kind of photography I had ever tried. Unlike normal image photography that is based on reflected light, Kirlian photography appears to record electromagnetic field changes of the human body or other living things directly onto film after stimulation of the subject by high-frequency, high-voltage, very-low-current electricity.

In addition to research by the Kirlians, work by Thelma Moss and Kendal Johnson at UCLA pioneered experiments with a low-frequency Kirlian device to study the energy bursts of biomagnetic healers who practiced so-called energy work on patients with their hands. Generally there is an almost symmetrical pattern to the energy bursts that are captured on film. The fingertips of biomagnetic healers in the UCLA experiments, however, showed decreases in the halo burst uniformity and size after healing.

I was interested in this sort of experiment with biomagnetic healers, too. I recruited subjects who had been working effectively in energy healing. What I discovered in subjecting them to electrical stimulation between the camera's electrode plates was that they could direct a flow of energy from their fingertips on command. They could make the bursts flow to the right or the left. They could concentrate the burst or spread it.

One of the famous Kirlian experiments that I was able to eventually replicate was the mysterious "lost leaf" photograph. The approach for the lost leaf photo was to sever one leaf of a plant and then photograph the phantom image of the severed member, which is evident in an energy burst that outlines the original physical form, as though still physically intact. I had unsuccessfully tried to capture the energy of a severed leaf on many occasions with my Kirlian partner, Mari Coryell. Her brother had actually constructed the camera for our experiments. Finally it dawned on us that we had never altered the duration between the severing of the leaf and our efforts to capture its lingering energy.

Energy changes everything. And we can measure real change brought about energetically with what we commonly call time. So we captured the severed leaf of a lucky shamrock plant with the Kirlian camera five seconds after plucking the leaf physically from the plant. What we discovered was that the energy field that surrounds all living things appears to break down after a very short duration.

What made me think that duration was the key was actually the fact that the Kirlians also had experimented with near-death scenarios. Apparently they would shock a human subject to near-death and then measure any changes in the body's weight before reviving the person. Weight loss of approximately one pound was reported in these experiments.

LIMITED PERCEPTION
AND OUSPENSKY'S OUTLOOK

In Eastern philosophy, which predates recorded Western thought by many centuries, sages long have viewed our physical world as the world of illusion or *maya*. This view suggests that we cannot trust our ideas or brains to accurately conceptualize reality, since things are not as they seem, physically speaking. To find real truth, Eastern sages look deeper by getting outside their bodies in higher consciousness, as seen in meditation. They do not trust their eyes, ears, or other physical sensations that are part of common perception. They learn to access higher consciousness by leaving their bodies and developing new awareness outside the physical senses.

P. D. Ouspensky considered the limitations of our sensory perception in his book *Tertium Organum*. The early Russian philosopher said we live a shallow existence, as though we are trapped in a box. In this confined situation, we have limited ways to perceive what is outside. He described our known dimensions as intersecting lines, with each line or plane containing a section of the plane above it. To understand this better, it might help to visualize floors in a high-rise building. Lower life-forms that live on the basement floor are unable to see things on the floors above them. Ouspensky uses this metaphor to show how lower life-forms are perhaps unable to perceive the same range of dimensions that people perceive. As a human being, you live on a higher floor of this building, yet you too are unable to see onto the floors above you. Ouspensky was talking about planes of existence. From our limited perspective, we cannot perceive the dimensions that might be available to beings on a higher plane of existence.

Many problems in perception arise from the inability to experience that which is outside of the dimensions in which a being lives. A one-dimensional being wouldn't notice anything on the plane above, even though that dimension also intersects its own little world. In fact, a one-dimensional being would probably perceive the higher plane as a phenomenon of the unknown world beyond its reality. The same would be true of a two-dimensional being whose plane is intersected by a third-dimensional line. This being cannot see beyond its own two-dimensional reality. The same, it would follow, would be true of people as three-dimensional beings who are unable to see beyond our three-dimensional reality, despite the possible close proximity of a fourth or even fifth dimension.

Ouspensky suggested that time might be considered our fourth dimension, but we live a very limited existence inside the physical boxes that we perceive to be the measurable walls of our reality. Most of us, sadly, are two-dimensional thinkers in a sort of flat "Etch A Sketch" world. As surface dwellers restricted to a three-dimensional reality, we cannot look deeply enough to see a fourth dimension or possible dimensions beyond that. Our inability to see beyond the surface of our known physical universe has always been a limitation. Our senses, perception, and frame of reference allow us to experience just three dimensions fully. Even our words for these three dimensions demonstrate that we are linear thinkers and material reductionists who define our world by measuring objects to the right and left, above and below.

In fact, we see in only two dimensions, with our inability to truly comprehend depth perhaps best demonstrated by our bafflement in confronting a cube. By our nature, we measure everything in our surroundings. We measure point A to point B. We measure up and down. The things we measure in our frame of reference are basically perpendicular angles. Sometimes we attempt to triangulate or show how three lines intersect. So we put the box on its side and measure again. We live in a little box and gain a small measure of confidence in controlling our environment by measuring things sideways, vertically, and in terms of depth, as we perceive it. This is how we experience reality.

It is difficult for three-dimensional beings like us to imagine additional dimensions. That is far different from saying that other dimensions don't exist. Rather, they are beyond our immediate grasp in our ordinary experience of reality. We are limited by our sensory receptors, our perception, and our experience in our existing frame of reference. We also have consciousness to experience our known reality, but most of us only employ normal consciousness and not the higher consciousness of what mystics who meditate deeply often call the higher mind.

But what if other realities were very close to us, just beyond the plane on which we live in our limited little boxes? I am reminded of an inventor who once told me that most people spend their lives lying on the ground without taking in the whole view of what is above or below. Few of us rise above our prone position. I challenge you to try the same experiment that the inventor made me try. In a secluded room, lie on your back beside a table filled with objects. From your position on the floor, try to describe the objects on the table above you. Now stand above the table to observe how much easier observation becomes for you. When I did this test in the inventor's living room, I had no idea from memory what items were on his table. And since the table was not transparent glass (so that I could cheat by seeing things on the table through the glass bottom), I was unable to name a single item accurately.

Ouspensky was one of the first Western researchers in Eastern mysticism to suggest that higher consciousness was the only legitimate way to explore and experience nonordinary reality beyond our limited physical perception. All serious physicists seem to concur that the important function of consciousness cannot be ignored in our attempts to explore the limits of reality. Ouspensky stated that consciousness can separate from the body and operate outside a material framework. In deep, exploratory meditation, a person in a state of heightened consciousness engages the higher mind and leaves the physical body and the limitations of this physical universe. A person in heightened awareness can explore beyond the senses, beyond normal perception, and beyond any cultural frame of reference. The boundaries of our known universe are not limitations at all to the higher mind and the meditator who seeks to explore alternate realities in the nonordinary world. In fact, the verification of alternate realities in alternate universes with added dimensions makes the possible adventure even more exciting to the meditator.

UNSEEN DIMENSIONS AND
OTHER REALITIES

Is there any hard evidence for parallel realities and additional dimensions outside a mystic's adventures into nonordinary reality? Science has always sought an answer to that question. Now many cutting-edge physicists believe that they have a positive answer. Physicists, of course, seek to create a picture of reality as we should see it outside ourselves. Their theories are naturally abstract, but are based on scientific research into the nature of things.

What some of the most celebrated modern physicists have to say about parallel worlds and added dimensions is really astounding. They say that parallel realities with added dimensions really do exist, but that they exist in entirely different universes. Furthermore, these uncharted universes run parallel to our known universe. They describe our universe as a rather flat place just around the bend from parallel universes, but limited basically to our three visible dimensions. That's the conclusion of several leading physicists who collaborated on a breakthrough article in *Scientific American* magazine titled "The Universe's Unseen Dimensions." The article was written by Nima Arkani-Hamed, Savas Dimopoulous, and Georgi Dvali.

These physicists see our entire three-dimensional universe as a sort of thin membrane floating in the full space of dimensions, possibly as many as ten dimensions in all. They maintain that invisible, parallel universes could coexist with ours on spatial membranes less than a millimeter from our own visible universe. A slightly different way of viewing this proximity, they say, is that these invisible, parallel universes might be simply different sheets of our own thin universe, *folded back on itself.* The big picture they describe looks like a folded road map. Our entire universe and our limited reality exist on one side of the folded map. On the other side of the map, a parallel universe exists just beyond our reach. In fact, they say that it might be correct to think of a road map folded several times, with many parallel universes and many added dimensions on the other side of the folds.

These cutting-edge physicists say that objects on the opposite side of our fold could appear very distant, even though they are not. Although we are very close to the other side, we are distant in the sense that light from one side of the fold could take billions of years to reach us as it works its way around the *folds in space*. This, too, could be a matter of restricted human perception.

LIMITED RANGE
OF OUR FIVE SENSES

As human beings, our perception of reality is limited by our physical senses, which are simply not as keen as they might be. Our ability to hear is not nearly as refined as that of dogs, for example. Our ability to see is not nearly as keen as that of cats. We cannot even smell as well as many other animals who share our physical, known world. We are inspired by the physical prowess of other animals that are faster, stronger, and have keener sensory perception than we have. As a result, we have emulated birds by building planes and emulated cheetahs by building fast cars. But we will never be truly catlike. We will never have the perspective of a giraffe. We cannot distinguish many shades and hues of color. We cannot hear many pitches of sound. So how can we really trust our eyes and ears? We are limited by our perceptive skills and the restrictions of our five senses.

Like a simple reflex camera, we see everything upside down and then seek to correct the image internally by turning it right side up in our heads. In fact, what we actually see with our eyes is simply a reflection of light bounced off objects. Then we seek to interpret what we have seen. How can we ever trust our eyes, once we consider all of this?

My cats once caught a rabbit in our enclosed backyard and dragged it in through their cat door. They hid the frightened, wounded creature in my laundry room behind the dryer. They would visit the laundry room, yet I never understood why they just stood there, staring at the dryer. That's because I could not see the rabbit behind the dryer. I could not smell the poor rabbit, even when it started to decompose. I would have attempted to rescue the injured rabbit, of course, but it just lay there dying for many days. Finally, when the air became absolutely rank, I noticed something unusual. I thought initially that it might be simply bad laundry smells. When I finally moved things to see what I could not see, it became painfully obvious that I had been oblivious to something another creature like a cat could easily notice.

If only we could see around corners and beyond the simple reflection of light off objects in our immediate surroundings, we might be able to perceive additional realities and added dimensions around the folds in space. And if we could see around the folds in space, perhaps we could see beyond the limited range of what we consider time in our physical, linear fashion. But light does not bend around right angles just for us, and we cannot see around corners. Hence, our universe and sense of reality is very limited.

CONSCIOUS PERCEPTION OF
A PAST AND FUTURE

It is nonetheless curious how many people seem to have past-life recall, déjà vu, or some sense that they have been somewhere or met someone before. It is also curious how many people have dreams or visions of the future, which later come true. There are various explanations for these phenomena. Some believe that we have all lived before in previous lives and occasionally meet someone we knew before in an earlier life. Some believe that a few people with accurate dreams or visions of the future have the rare gift of prophecy. Theosophists like Madame Blavatsky believed that our consciousness lives outside of our physical body and has knowledge beyond what the physical brain knows in its limited capacity. Furthermore, she believed that we have conscious awareness in every cell of our body, as our consciousness inhabits us in this physical life of ours.

That might be an explanation for "remembered pain" of blocked memories that a myofascial therapist can trigger in unwinding sessions by touching various parts of the physical body. Research described by Robert B. Stone in *The Secret Life of Your Cells* notes how we seem to have a conscious awareness within every cell of our body, which extends to events that have impacted other cells in the body. This is very similar to Cleve Backster's discovery discussed in *The Secret Life of Plants,* where he found an emotional connection between plants that had been separated after having been close in proximity to each other. Working with two such plants, he attached a polygraph to each and then measured the emotional response of one plant when the other plant (some distance away) was threatened with damage. Backster also has reported a similar conscious connection in experiments with common chicken eggs that were separated out of a carton. The egg that was not in danger nonetheless showed emotional distress on Backster's polygraph when the other egg from the carton—then a mile away—was threatened with danger.

We all have read numerous accounts of people who were temporarily dead or unconscious, yet seemed to have conscious awareness of what happened outside of their bodies when they were physically gone. There seems to be a common thread to these anecdotes. The consciousness seems to hover over the physical body and look down on on it in an out-of-body experience.

When we consider how many people seem to know instinctively who is calling before picking up the phone or know when someone is approaching their door, we begin to sense that we have a conscious awareness that exists outside the realm of our physical senses and the frame of reference stored in the brain. How are we able to predict the future in this way? Do the past, present, and future truly exist simultaneously for us, as Einstein suggested?

TIME AS A SPINNING WHEEL

Time, as we seem to experience it, might be viewed as a spinning wheel that twirls and twirls in a way that captures our fascination. We are entranced by the whirl of the wheel as it spins, seemingly wobbling out of control. This is our illusion. In reality, however, we may be encased inside a wheel of change or a wheel of karma* that spins round and round, with us anchored at its hub.

At the center of even a wobbly wheel is a quiet, still point around which everything revolves. So it is with us. At the center of our being is a quiet, inner still point. Everything revolves around it. Call it our inner life force. Or call it our consciousness. When we access this still point deep within us, we can transcend the illusions around us and rise above the limitations of the physical realm.

Once we take control of the wheel that spins our lives and then focus our attention squarely on the outer spokes that are spinning, we begin to control time. Once we gain this level of certainty, we are no longer spinning out of control. We become masters of time and space, able to live in cocreative harmony in an expanded universe. The exercises that follow will help you to experience this possibility for yourself.

> **Note:** You may want to record yourself reading the instructions for the meditations given in the exercise procedures in the book and then follow them as you listen to the playback. If you do so, be sure to allow silent pauses between the steps.

BEGINNING MEDITATION OUTSIDE TIME

What You Need
- A quiet, secure room where you can close the door for privacy, if possible.
- A mat, blanket, or towel to allow you to lie on the floor.
- Loose-fitting clothes that do not constrain you in any way (remove shoes).

---

*Do not think of karma simply as scales of blind justice that dispense punishments or rewards for decisions made in one lifetime with some sort of personal compensation in the future. Instead, think of karma as nature's unerring balancing act to measure cause and effect. Karma, as it affects all living things in an orderly universe, acts as a moral law to restore order, balance, harmony, and opportunity for right action.

Procedure

1. Lie on your back in a comfortable position with legs separated and arms out to your sides approximately forty-five degrees from your torso (approximating yoga's "dead man" posture).

2. With lights on, allow your eyes to close most of the way, with a little light trickling in through your eyelashes.

3. Allow your physical body to become relaxed and numb, focusing if necessary on each part of your body, from your toes to your nose, as you allow it to become heavy and go to sleep.

4. Begin deep, controlled breathing through your nostrils, inhaling for approximately three seconds, holding the oxygen in your lungs for approximately three seconds, and then slowly exhaling for approximately three seconds. As you do this, consider the energy in the air all around you and now inside you. Exhale this energized air with your blessing into the world around you.

5. Consciously shut down all unnecessary sensory awareness, tuning out the sounds, smells, and other sensations that you might have of the physical world around you.

6. Consciously tune out all internal dialogue and chatter, suspending your reflections on past events and concerns about future events. End all internal thought and focus your consciousness on a blank slate in your mind's eye.

7. Go deep within yourself to the center of your being to connect with your inner spirit and life force.

8. Notice the sense of peace and joy that comes to you as you connect to your inner life force in a state of heightened consciousness.

9. Notice how you are fully experiencing the present moment and all of its potential, connected as you are with your inner spirit and energy essence.

10. Observe how the blank slate in your mind's eye is a perfectly white tableau.

11. Observe how time and space appear to dissolve in this state of heightened consciousness, as you fully occupy the present moment and experience timelessness and infinite potential.

12. When you are ready to return to your physical presence in normal consciousness, focus your attention on your body, beginning with your toes and working your way up your body to restore your physical sensations. When normal feeling has returned to your physical body, slowly open your eyes.

13. Cautiously return to your feet in a standing position, first making certain that all routine physical sensation has returned to your body and that routine consciousness has resumed.

14. Recapitulate and assess what you have experienced and the sensation of being outside normal physical space and time.

HEALING YOURSELF FROM THE OUTSIDE

What You Need
- A safe, secure room in which to meditate.
- Loose-fitting clothing, with shoes removed.
- A mat, pad, blanket, or towel on which to lie on your back, with legs and arms slightly apart from the body.

Procedure
1. Reclining on your back with limbs extended slightly, tune out all external and internal distractions and go deep within yourself to find a still, quiet point where spirit resides.

2. Breathe deeply and slowly through your nostrils, focusing on the energy in the air as you inhale, hold it, and then expel it with your blessing.

3. As your body grows heavy and numb, let it go to sleep, as your higher consciousness races faster and faster.

4. Allow your consciousness to rise from your physical body and hover over your physical self within the room.

5. As you look down on your physical self in your raised consciousness, observe any physical, mental, emotional, or spiritual illness or anomaly. Then send healing thought-forms to that point of concern.

6. Slowly return your consciousness to your physical body and begin to feel normal bodily sensations.

7. When it seems right to you, slowly open your eyes and sit upright.

8. Recapitulate what you have experienced in this out-of-body healing meditation and reflect on the new conscious awareness that you enjoyed in higher consciousness with new eyes and new ways to observe.

9. Reflect on how you experienced timelessness and new energy potential outside the body.

Second Secret of Time

POWER IN THE PRESENT MOMENT

Eastern mystics for centuries have taught yoga students how to meditate to become one with the Eternal Now. That concept has spread worldwide to wherever serious people meditate. It is an essential part of the yoga training of American Ram Dass, author of the classic manual *Be Here Now.* It evolved into workshops on *The Power of Now,* a popular book by Eckert Tolle. It was also a big part of the message of the English-American philosopher and religious scholar Alan Watts, who introduced Westerners to Eastern philosophies and particularly Zen Buddhism through his many books, instructional tapes, and television programs. He believed that he was sort of an advance man for a great teacher who would come out of the East to bring people to a higher level of consciousness. He encouraged people to live in the Now. Curiously, he became the teacher that he had envisioned.

That new world teacher also could have been the Indian sage Jiddu Krishnamurti, an author and world-renowned lecturer on Eastern philosophy. Before dissolving his worldwide organization and encouraging his many followers to become their own teacher and find the truth for themselves, Krishnamurti predicted a great awakening of consciousness. He believed that most people who live a drab life of work, eat, and sleep, with thoughts no deeper than supplying creature comforts, were sleep-walking through life, not totally awake. He called for an awakening of higher consciousness. To make that possible, he taught meditation.

MEDITATE TO BECOME ONE WITH THE ALL

In the Eastern tradition, to learn to truly meditate to become one with all or attain union with the eternal infinite, a person tunes out inner worries about the future and reflections on the past. Concerns about what has happened and what might happen to us unfortunately preoccupy our minds most of the time. Consequently, meditation training helps to focus a person's consciousness only on the present moment or the Now.

As we have seen, from physicist Julian Barbour's perspective, that instant is all that really exists, at least in our physical realm. Anything else is pure speculation, a fancy of the mind. We cannot touch the past or affect the future from where we sit in the present moment. Anyone who's ever tried to overcome addiction through Alcoholics Anonymous knows the mantra, "One day at a time," and the Serenity Prayer, which goes:

> God grant us the serenity to accept the things we cannot change, the courage to change the things we can, and the wisdom to know the difference.

Where we sit in the here and now, the past is long gone and beyond our control. The future is only a vision of tomorrow, also beyond our immediate control. We live in the moment. Those who understand this simple fact take some measure of control over their lives and make the most of their opportunity by not fretting about other times beyond their immediate grasp.

Many people have difficulty meditating because they believe that they are unable to let go of their concerns about the past and worries about an uncertain future. Consequently, they cannot still the clutter in their heads to focus on the Now. In the East this lack of control is sometimes called "monkey mind" since the internal dialogue resembles frenetic monkey chatter.

Learning to still the inner mind means focusing your conscious attention entirely on the Now. Similar to self-hypnosis, meditation requires a suspension of sensory overload, internal dialogue, and preoccupation with outside physical distractions, a numbing of physical feeling, and a singular focus on going deeper inside oneself to find inner stillness and silence. In short, we put the physical body to sleep, while the conscious mind begins racing at new speeds, freed from physical limitations. When we slow down the outer, physical world and go within ourselves in this fashion, we begin to experience the present moment more fully.

For most people, this deeper experience with the present moment is the closest they will ever get to experiencing timelessness or even time shifts. They might focus on the emptiness of space, looking into a blank, dark void outside the material world that awaits their meaningful exploration. Out of this darkness, answers may come. The Eternal Now fills them with the full potential of the present moment. They gain traction in a way they had never experienced in the physical world, with all of its limitations and illusions about reality. They leave behind the false hopes of personally touching the past or future from where we physically stand on this revolving sphere of mud and water.

Many people also find it personally difficult to meditate because they have a limited idea of meditation. To some people, the concept of meditation has been reduced to reflection, quiet time alone, personal introspection, or even a different way of praying with healing, loving, and insightful thoughts. Some people believe that they can't reach deeper, more meaningful meditation states, because they are unable to tune out all outer and inner distractions or because the world around them seems just too noisy. Krishnamurti chastised people who blamed their inability to meditate on noisy children and other outer disturbances, reminding them that it should be possible to meditate anywhere in any condition. You are not dependent on ideal conditions around you to find the opportunity to meditate. You are dependent only on your own resolve and singular focus to tune out the physical world and its trappings to find an inner stillness.

Many people who want to meditate resort to gadgets and tricks, such as a dot on the wall or a sound struck on a triangle or metal bowl. But meditation is really not hypnotism, where an outside agent takes control of you. In meditation, you take control of yourself and focus your attention. You think of nothing. You turn off your physical brain. You numb your body. You put it to sleep. What is left is your consciousness, a level of personal awareness outside your body or your brain. It is your higher self.

Strangely, it's frightening for many people to release their higher self. Switching off physical controls and allowing your body and lower, analytical mind to go to sleep can sound threatening. The physical side of you naturally wants to maintain control because it wants to remain in charge. After all, it is responsible for your physical safety. Its highest function is physical survival and protection from outside threats. In meditation, however, the change agent comes not from outside us, but deep inside us where higher consciousness resides. This is our spirit, our essential life force, and our energy center. And our spirit longs to be free to explore and grow. Its natural responsibility is our spiritual evolution. It is what connects us with the spirit in all and the life force energy of the universe.

REACHING INNER HARMONY

For deep meditation we must be in total accord and at peace within, free from the feeling of threat that the physical body may feel as its control is relaxed. We can resolve this dilemma by comforting our physical side with the assurance that our bodies will be safely tucked away in restful repose during meditation. You might want to meditate on this very bargain to strike an accord between body and spirit to safely release your higher consciousness. Think of it as being like negotiating for hostages and their safe passage. With this agreement, there would be accord within you as you approach meditation. The lower mind—your physical brain—is very analytical. It will respond to reason. Your higher consciousness can assure your physical self that it will be safe in a restful position. That's why we recommend a quiet, safe room where you will not be disturbed as the ideal meditation site. There the physical body will remain warm, dry, and protected. Reclining on your back with arms and legs comfortably outstretched also guarantees that your body will lie in gentle repose that will be restful for the brief period during which your physical self surrenders control to your higher consciousness.

When we meditate, we seek to fully occupy the present moment. We do this by tuning out all thoughts about the past and the future as concepts and projections. We recognize that we are frozen in the present moment, this instant where light as energy has touched us to empower us.

This is like catching a big wave. If you have ever stood on the beach and observed waves crashing toward you on the shore, you have noticed that there is a succession of waves. Each wave, however, meets you on the beach in its own time. This represents its instant in time, the Now. There is tremendous power in a wave as it realizes its moment for striking the shore. The wave can crash with awesome power against you, as well, as you position yourself at this instant in time. A wave that already has passed does not impact you. The successive waves that have not reached the shore and you standing there do not impact you. Only the wave of the moment crashes into you with power. As you stand in front of it at a given place and time, you feel the energy of the wave at the instant it strikes you.

There is energy in many forms in the natural world around us. All of the energy, however, resides in the present moment or instant when energy strikes you. When we bask in the light of day, empowered by the radiant energy of sunlight that shines down with unceasing love, the light strikes all of us at different instants. You can see this in the early morning when the rising sun creeps along the horizon. As the morning sun strikes each living thing in time, the radiant energy energizes all. At the moment that this electromagnetic radiation touches each living thing, it invigorates and rejuvenates. And this is the power of the present moment, the Now.

OTHER ANIMALS LIVE INSTINCTIVELY IN THE MOMENT

Other animals who share our physical world seem to live more naturally in the moment than we do. Perhaps it's because they do not try to live inside their heads, with thoughts stuck in the past and the future. They are not preoccupied by thoughts of more than the present moment. They are not burdened with our sort of endless mind games that resemble a trip through a maze.

Have you ever observed how a flock of birds in flight will all turn uniformly at once? Like most animals, they are able to live instinctively in the moment. Assume that you are one of those birds in flight. Imagine that you are flashing through the sky in formation. You do not have random reflections about your past concerns as a burden on your conscious attention. You are not projecting what problems or challenges might await you tomorrow or next week. You are totally living in the moment, meeting the energy that presents itself at this instant. You are totally alert, awake, and aware. You have a conscious awareness that makes your focus keen and tuned into your immediate surroundings in the moment at hand.

People who have shared their life and home with a cat as a companion are familiar with how these animals live in the moment. While cats appear to sleep sixteen or more hours each day, you have probably noticed that they always have one eye half open and are ready to spring to life. In fact, their state of repose might be more accurately described as meditation or lucid dreaming, because they rarely spring from repose in a drowsy condition. To the contrary, they appear highly conscious even during repose, always living in the moment. We might add that cats are famous for always finding the sunniest spot to recline, always looking for the most energy in any setting. They will often circle a room or area for some time, as though carefully selecting their power spot.

Animals—apart from the human species—live by keen awareness, measured by their sensory perception. They are immediately tuned into new smells, new sights, and new sounds. They are attuned to the changes in nature. If we want to know what's happening to our weather at the moment, we look to the animals around us for their immediate response to what is happening around us. Meanwhile, we are lost inside our heads and preoccupied by sorting through old bills or planning activities for next week.

We tend to refer to this greater alertness of other animals as "animal instinct." Maybe we should call it "living in the moment, fully focused with conscious awareness on the opportunities of the present." This is not to say that animals apart from humans are shallow in their thoughts or simpleminded. Groups of elephants grieve for their departed members, as witnessed by their sojourns to burial grounds and somber behavior once they arrive. Schools of fish accompany members in trouble. During travel, killer whales stop to play and care for the group's youngsters and even shield weakened pod members by supporting them on all sides with their own bodies. Many critters nurse and care for all of the young, regardless of parenthood. Sentry bees stand guard at the entrance of the hive until death overcomes them. Even snakes curl together. We might one day be forced to admit that humans are not the only consciously aware beings in our world and not even the most highly evolved.

Animals live closer to nature than we do, engaged in the moment when a flower opens to meet the sun and the moon casts its power on tides and creatures of the night. Since the essential spirit of creation resides in nature, we might consider how animals that live all of their lives close to nature have a greater sense of true spirituality than people. They can realize the true meaning of life because they walk hand in hand with the spirit of nature. Their world is the world of earth, sky, and water and not the world of asphalt, roofed enclosures, and carbonated beverages that defines our pitiful existence.

In contrast to other animals, people like to think about themselves and their capacity to analyze. We seem to love the fact that we have a physical brain that enables us to conceptualize. We think of ourselves as outside the animal kingdom, as the one self-aware creature with great reasoning ability. Many people regard humans as exalted beings who stand supremely outside the natural world, self-aware, self-realized, and conscious. Perhaps we would do better to label human beings as self-conscious beings who see the world inside their heads with little effort to integrate themselves with the natural world around them.

I like to refer to our physical, analytical brain as our little pocket organizer. It promises to sort everything out for us with great precision, yet it only concerns itself with small thoughts that mostly focus on itself and its own petty concerns about controlling things. It does not live focused in the present moment, where power resides. It seems to believe that it controls our destiny by measuring things for us. It also does its best to measure us in all situations, including the past and the future. But the past is gone, and the future is only speculation. In truth, we cannot control many things in our world from where we stand. We can only rise up to meet the world by living fully in the present moment when the light of day strikes us. This is our moment. This is our opportunity for action.

THE REAL HERO SEIZES THE MOMENT

The ancient Hindu classic, *The Bhagavad Gita,* considers what makes a real hero. It's not the person who worries about the past or future. It's not the person who frets over the downside of every action. It's not the person who avoids decisions and fears making bad choices. It's the man or woman who takes action when needed and gets involved in the surrounding world. It teaches us that we cannot live our lives safely hidden away from danger and the possibility of making bad choices. We must be fully engaged and seize the moment.

Arjuna, the warrior hero in *The Bhagavad Gita,* also known as *The Song of the Lord*, expresses his concerns to the Lord that he fears making mistakes in his participation in a battle. This battle represents life. Our hero frets that he could confuse right action with wrong action in a battle for good over evil. What seems like right action could have the wrong effect. The very thought of fighting could be considered wrong action for the right reason. And so a would-be hero could easily make mistakes and incur bad karma for himself. Arjuna, faced with unavoidable challenge, contemplates his future based on actions he might take in the moment at hand. The Lord, however, advises him to be a man of action, engaging in the immediate world around him.

All of us are a lot like Arjuna. Our physical self, with its little pocket-calculator-size brain, sizes up the potential dangers around us and worries about our future. It analyzes the situation and cautions safety, avoiding jumping into live action that is unfolding immediately before us. This is our great opportunity, however, to seize the moment and free our spirit to engage in the power of the present.

TIME IS ENERGY AND OPPORTUNITY

Perhaps, then, we should begin to consider time as energy of the moment and consider the opportunity it presents for us in the here and now. After all, we know that energy comes to us in waves. If we consider nature all around us as our teacher, it offers us a bounty of examples of how creation works. The power of the present moment is the wave on the beach just as it reaches us or the gust of wind that hits us in the face. Future waves are just rumors of what might come our way. Past waves are behind us, with no immediate impact on our present condition.

Every person who has ridden waves in the surf knows the opportunities provided by the power of a wave when you fully engage with it. If you catch the wave perfectly, it can give you a wonderful ride. However, the surfer who misses the wave often is blindsided and taken on a disruptive tumble.

Many shamanic cultures attempt to live in the moment, close to nature, like the rest of the natural kingdom. Their folk religions have traditionally viewed nature, energy, and spirit as one. I recall a teacher friend in Alaska telling me just how hard it was for teachers coming from elsewhere to impress on Inuit school children the need to do homework or prepare for a test "tomorrow." The concept of *tomorrow* was somewhat foreign to the young pupils' worldview and awareness of how things really work in the natural world.

This is consistent with the view of time described by Einstein's special theory of relativity, which considers the precise instant when sunlight strikes each one of us. This is the present moment, the instant of empowerment. This is when energy is transformed from an unmanifest state outside our physical reality to manifest in the physical world, where we can readily use it. Energy that has become manifest is a gift from the heavens, a gift from God. Such a gift should be readily received with our full attention. Arjuna learned this truth, and it made him a happier and more effective person.

SOLAR TIME

Physicist Julian Barbour in *The End of Time* was certainly not the first person to observe that solar time is the only time on earth. Traditional folk religions often celebrated the sun and its reflections in the moon with festivals to mark this creative force in their immediate lives and how it impacted them differently throughout the seasons. These ancients honored the immediate presence of the sun all throughout the year, mindful of its present location and the intensity of its rays from day to day. In many ongoing wisdom traditions, such as Theosophy and astrology, the sun is honored as more than a sphere in our sky, as the Solar Logos or Father Sun. Ancient religions worshipped the sun. Even today, much has been written comparing the son of God to the sun of God.

Our sun provides the energy and creative opportunity for all growth and activities on earth. Consequently, sundials measured real time. A clock that counts off twenty-four hours as the standard day is certainly not accurate, since some days are shorter than others, depending on the season and how the light strikes you at a given place on the globe. To state this scientifically, less energy pours down on the earth in the form of electromagnetic radiation (light) on some days than other days, as we measure sunrise to sunset at various times of the year in different parts of our world, as our world spins and rotates around the sun. That's the realistic truth. You might think that you can squeeze more hours out of the day by carrying around a digital watch, but you're only kidding yourself. When the sun sets, flowers fold and forest creatures recognize day's end. If you try to live outside of nature, you will be out of harmony with the spirit of nature, fall prey to darkness, and possibly suffer anxiety. You will become the lost soul who dreams of tomorrows that have not yet materialized.

Sunlight is refracted in a prismatic effect as it curves to bend down to earth, falling on our physical world in a spectrum effect with seven basic colors that we are able to perceive in nature. These are the seven colors of the rainbow. And each color of light has specific, unique properties based on the frequency of its energy wave band. Consequently, all light is not the same, but unique, with various characteristics. Pagan farmers, living close to nature, recognized this when they considered the predominant color of the sun and moon throughout the growing year.

AGENTS OF CHANGE

If we learn to live in harmony with the rhythm of nature, we are living in the creative moment at the instant when energy reaches us with the greatest intensity and opportunity. If we can become one with the energy at this instant, we can join with it and be empowered by it. Our creative spirit can become one with the creative spirit in the manifest energy. This makes us potential agents of change. With this approach to living, we are not fated pawns in the game of life, awaiting our destiny on the wheel of karma. We take control of our karma by living like Arjuna, a hero of action who controls his own karma and destiny. We are no longer idle victims of waves that hit us unaware, but action figures who ride the waves at the moment they arrive. We become agents of change in harmonic balance with the forces around us.

Agents of change control their own destiny. They are people of power, heroes who take immediate action. They are able to transcend the physical laws of our manifest world. They become energized transformers, dynamos who have been awakened to their full potential to absorb, process, and amplify energy. They take control of their lives and the obstacles that seem to prevent most of us from healing. They become *transcendent,* so that what is physically broken or broken on some other level in this frozen, manifest world can be mended. They no longer live on the outer spokes of the wheel of life and the wheel of karma, spinning dizzily out of control, but take a hub position at the still point in the center. No longer dizzy from the wild, spinning ride, they stand at the heart of the action. The following exercises will guide you toward becoming an agent of change.

CATCHING THE WIND

What You Need

- An area where you can feel wind that is gusting toward you. Ideally this will be a quiet, open area where you can be alone to experience the wind.
- Comfortable, loose-fitting clothing for standing outdoors in the wind. (No clothing should cover your face.)
- Select a day when you can stay outside for a while to experience wind action.

Procedure

1. Determine the direction of the wind and then stand facing it.
2. Remain quiet and still.
3. Clear your mind of internal thought and external distractions, focusing only on the wind as it strikes you.
4. Do not anticipate. Just allow each new gust of wind to reach you and experience it as it arrives.
5. Begin to notice how each gust of wind is slightly different and that you cannot always determine the pattern or strength of the various gusts of wind that blow your way.

CATCHING THE WAVE

What You Need

• Find a shore at the ocean, a river, or a large lake with an incoming tide or with boat waves that wash ashore in a series.

Procedure

1. Remain quiet and still as you stand at the water's edge, facing the waves. It would be ideal to stand ankle deep in the water with your shoes removed.
2. Clear your mind of internal thought and external distractions, focusing only on the waves as they reach you.
3. Do not anticipate. Just experience each new wave as it reaches you.
4. Begin to notice how each wave is slightly different and that you cannot always determine the pattern or strength of the various waves, particularly with incoming tides.

STANDING IN THE LIGHT

What You Need

• Find a place to stand to greet the rising sun at first dawn. (This could be a life-changing experience if you have never witnessed a sunrise with full attention.)
• Comfortable, loose-fitting clothing. (Nothing should cover your face.)

Procedure

1. Remain quiet and still as you stand facing the direction of the rising sun. It would be ideal, if weather permits, to stand with bare feet and as little clothing as possible.

2. Clear your mind of internal thoughts and external distractions, focusing only on the sun as it reaches you.

3. Do not anticipate. Just allow yourself to be in the moment, fully experiencing the new dawn and feeling the warmth and power of the sun as it envelops your body.

4. Begin to notice how the sun glows brighter from moment to moment and how every plant around you becomes energized when the sun first reaches it.

Recapitulation

• Did you notice that your experience varied from moment to moment in these experiments, as the energy struck you and things around you?

• Did your heightened consciousness and focused attention in these exercises enable you to experience new power in the present moment, as the energy touched you?

• Did you experience a sense of joining with the energy forces in nature or a oneness with the creative life forces?

• Did you feel more alive than usual in these experiences?

• Did time seem to stand still for you?

3

Third Secret of Time

TIME = ENERGY = OPPORTUNITY = KARMA

I have personally experienced the power of the present moment. It was the time I nearly died in a crash.

I would wager that you have had similar experiences. We have all probably lived through special moments when time seemed to stand still. To be sure, such special moments in our memory are often scary situations. They are always, however, cloaked in opportunity. These are usually critical moments when we are forced to really focus our attention to cope with the situation in front of us. Maybe you have experienced this stretching of time during an accident, crisis, or intense danger. Maybe it was a very wonderful moment. In these instances, we fully occupy the present moment, with all of its potential power.

The time of my near-fatal accident in my little Triumph sports car was in the early 1970s when I worked for a community newspaper in Anacortes, Washington. I was racing down a hill on a sunny day, coming down toward the town of Anacortes below. I expected, as usual, that I would be able to make the turns on good pavement, even on the hairpin turn that loomed ahead at the bottom of the hill. What I did *not* realize, however, was that it had rained on that side of the hill just the night before, leaving a big puddle of collected water at the bottom where I needed to turn hard left. I was going pretty fast, not expecting any problem. I realized at almost the last instant that I would hydroplane in the deep puddle of water at the bottom of the hill. I would not be able to make the hard left turn at my rate of speed. In short, I would skid out of control on the water.

The bottom of this hill overlooked a cliff, with Fidalgo Bay far below. The cliff was blocked with a metal guard rail. So it appeared that, if I were unable to turn on a dime where the puddle had formed, I would crash into the guard rail or else crash through the guard rail and plunge over the cliff.

That is when I began to experience the power of the present moment. I felt my spirit leaving my body and my higher consciousness taking control. This higher mind was racing very quickly, so that everything around me seemed to be in slow motion. I was extremely focused.

I had probably only two seconds before I hit the pool of water. When I entered a state of heightened consciousness, however, time seemed to stand still. I was able to rapidly consider various possible solutions to my problem. I'd never encountered this sort of problem before, so I considered many things. I thought about my little car racing toward the hairpin turn and my need to respond immediately and decisively. I considered downshifting, but figured that would not slow the car soon enough. I considered braking hard, but figured that could throw me into an uncontrolled skid at the wet bottom of the hill. I considered turning off the engine, but figured that wouldn't slow me enough and would rob me of any control of the car.

Then, without panic, I calmly decided what to do. I would shift all the way down to first gear, cramp the steering wheel hard to the left when I reached the bottom of the hill, and then floor the gas pedal to try to spin the tires to catch whatever pavement they could catch through the water. Miraculously, my plan worked. The little sports car spun around to the left, merely grazing the metal barrier that blocked the cliff embankment. After negotiating the turn, I returned to a normal, if somewhat bewildered, state of consciousness and drove around aimlessly through back alleys in the town for awhile. I finally parked in an alley to sit and ponder. A policeman drove up to me to ask if I was the guy who had grazed the barrier up the hill.

When I have told this story, which first appeared in my earlier book *Perfect Timing,* people in workshops and on radio call-in shows have often shared very similar stories about special moments in their lives. These were usually in crisis situations. They almost always would describe a sense of getting outside their bodies, with heightened consciousness and focused awareness in the present moment. These are life-changing experiences in time perception. Speaking only for myself and my near-fatal crash with the Triumph, I believe I was awakened at the critical instant. It was my epiphany or "ah-ha!" experience that changed everything for me.

JUMPING OUT OF YOUR BODY

My son also had a special moment of this sort when we were on a bicycle trip across Vancouver Island in beautiful British Columbia one late summer afternoon. Together we shared one racing bike and one slower bike, so we took turns riding the twelve-speed European racer.

During one of my son's turns on the fast bike, he pulled ahead of me to enter the highway. He signaled to turn and then got into the bike lane at the far right of the highway with the sort of bike safety that we always followed. Out of nowhere a drunk driver sped around me to enter the highway, too, swerving wildly to the right of the road. He was heading directly into my son, as though he didn't even see him there. My son didn't have much warning of the car overtaking him from the rear. I covered my eyes and cried out in horror. When I looked up again, I could scarcely believe my eyes.

My son put his weight on the handle bars and did a sort of gymnastic leapfrog move to hop over the front of his bike, just as the car was crashing into the rear of the bike. After he cleared the bike, my son landed perfectly flat on the ground, parallel to the road. As a result, the car drove over him without hurting him. The bike was totaled. To this day, I can't believe what I saw.

When I asked my son how he'd made his amazing and quick escape from almost certain death, he just mumbled something about everything moving in slow motion and seeing things from outside his body.

LEARNING TIME MANIPULATION

Years later, I found that I could stretch or manipulate time in much the same way whenever situations demanded it. It was simply a matter of getting back into the same state of consciousness as when I was facing the watery hairpin turn by focusing my awareness on the moment and getting outside myself. This proved handy later when I was trying to put out a small community newspaper with no backup staff on a wonderful little island in Alaska. The deadlines were killers. I would need to gather all of the ads, then the news, then the photographs, then the classifieds, then typeset and paste together pages, and then rush those composite pages out to the next plane or state ferry to make the deadline on the presses of a daily newspaper plant on a neighboring island. I also had to send out all of the bills, keep track of distribution, and maintain records.

The one-man project required the wearing of many hats, and each hat carried its own tight deadlines. So I tried to "stretch" time, making the present moment last longer for me. As I'd learned in my near fatality with the sports car only a couple of years earlier, this meant focusing my attention on the present moment, tuning out all internal noise and external sensory clutter, and reaching a state of heightened consciousness. It's amazing what you can accomplish when your spirit or life force works in harmony with the rest of your body. In the case of my island newspaper deadlines, I was able to enter a personal "zone," a state of flow, where I could accomplish an hour's worth of work in minutes.

I recall one night when I was behind and needed to assemble all of my pages by 4 a.m. to put them on the morning ferry at 4:30. There was twice as much work as I could normally handle in such little time, especially with no rest. What was remarkable was that I was asleep on my feet, yet accomplishing everything in record time. I had put most of my body to sleep, while entering a heightened state of awareness. I had the use of my hands, but later remembered very little about the work. This must be the way star batters in baseball slow down the ball in their mind's eye and all-star basketball players see fast-moving, complex plays on the court developing very slowly in front of their eyes. They get into a zone.

STRETCHING TIME ACROSS ALL OF MONTANA

When I sold my island newspaper in beautiful Petersburg, Alaska, I drove across Montana one cold winter day on my way to Wyoming. I didn't realize how large Montana was when I started across the state in the wee hours of the morning. It was during a blizzard and very cold. I saw no signs of roadside inns or hotels to stop for the night. I saw no gas stations that were open that early. I was nearly out of gas in my Ford Bronco. So I kept moving forward across Big Sky Country.

To survive and not run out of gas in an early-morning blizzard in the middle of nowhere, I decided to stretch the time that my short supply of fuel would last. So I entered a state of heightened consciousness, as I had learned a few years earlier. I focused my attention fully on the present moment. It feels a little strange to drive a car when you are in this state (and I don't recommend it, because it could be dangerous). I felt that I was somewhere outside my body, which was still functioning. I did not feel my body, but my hands were on the wheel, my foot on the gas pedal, and my eyes on the road. Other than that, I felt totally alienated from my physical form.

When I started to do this, my gas gauge read almost down to "E" for empty. About two or three hours later, the gas gauge hadn't moved. I say this was about two or three hours later, although time seemed to stand still. I can only judge that two or three normal hours of driving had elapsed, because I was almost across Montana, with the sun coming up. My manipulation of time hadn't impacted the rest of Big Sky Country, but it had impacted me in the Bronco, with its nearly empty fuel tank.

MOVING FREELY THROUGHOUT TIME

Another favorite story about time manipulation in a state of heightened consciousness involves my mother. When she was a girl back on the family farm in North Dakota, one summer day she saw a young man who looked out of place in his white dress shirt. He was walking across a livestock pen in back of the house toward a gate. He did not seem to notice anyone around him, even though my mother waved at him. She thought she recognized him in a way. He looked like her younger brother, only he appeared to be years older than her brother, who would have been only ten years old at that time. The man's face was similar, however, and his wavy, black hair looked the same to her, too. He even whistled the same way her brother whistled. But when he opened the gate and walked through it, he just vanished in front of her eyes.

Now this incident did not make much sense to my mother until she was much older. Years later, she could identify the young man without hesitation. That man looked just the way her younger brother looked when he grew up, went to war, and died of tuberculosis shortly after coming home from the Navy. His white shirt was the last thing she saw him wear when he visited her on the West Coast. He died shortly after that, never making it back to the old homestead in North Dakota. Or did he? It always seemed to my mother that he chose to go back to his first home the way he remembered it as a boy. He had returned to his past one last time.

There is no limitation or constraint outside this material world. Spirit is not restricted. Our consciousness is not restricted. We can step outside our physical forms and move freely outside space and time, where the future, present, and past are one interconnected loop, without beginning and without end.

OPPORTUNITY AND KARMA

As we have learned, what we generally call time is really energy at the instant it touches us. We can realize that as an opportunity if we are totally awake and aware. If we seize our opportunity with the personal power of the present moment, then we can control our karma. After all, karma is simply the opportunity to learn, grow, change, and evolve spiritually.

Opportunity is always drawn to us. We have many opportunities to act responsibly to deal with the many challenges of our lives. Opportunity comes to us in many forms to energize us. It comes as a wave, a gust of wind, or a ray of sunlight. If we are awake and consciously aware, we will seize each opportunity.

Opportunities vary from instant to instant, of course. You need to recognize the unique quality of each new opportunity. Deep down inside us, we all seem to sense that each new dawn brings unique opportunity. Our spirit recognizes the difference. If you reflect on your energy level and impulses yesterday and the day before yesterday, you will begin to recognize the changing tides of opportunity. If you have studied divination techniques such as astrology, numerology, tarot, runes, or the I Ching, you already have a working understanding about the changing tides of opportunity. One day when you step into the sunlight, you might sense that it's the perfect day to take a trip. The next day when you step into the sunlight, you sense that it's the perfect day to sort out your finances. Every day the new sunrise strikes you with new energy and new opportunity to do what you need to do. Hopefully, you will be able to read and use the energy at the moment it presents itself to you to do what you really need to do.

There is a general confusion over the meaning of karma in the West and even sometimes in the East, where the concept originated. Karma is often thought to be something like justice or repercussion. Many people think of it like balancing scales, whereby your actions result in karma in the form of punishment. Some people think of a hall of justice where our karma is determined and meted out by Lords of Karma like some sort of comic book League of Justice. Others think of karma like fate that we encounter, often unknowingly. Others consider our encounter with karma like stepping into cow dung in a big, open pasture. Certainly, there could be an element of truth to all of these ideas. But karma is really opportunity for right action, a great opportunity for all of us and hardly a harsh, insensitive punishment. Karma weighs all of our actions and works to establish balance and order in a universe that naturally strives toward harmony. We all are responsible for our own karma, and we create karma as we live. But remember the story of Arjuna, the hero in the classic Hindu story *The Bhagavad Gita*. Like Job, Arjuna argues with God and attempts to determine the limits of his responsibility.

Arjuna represents the common person, because all of us are potential heroes. The hero's journey takes the individual through many life challenges filled with opportunity. In literature, this is sometimes called the hero's triumph and return home. Like Ulysses, we are all on a life journey that is filled with challenges, trying to find our way around the world and back home again. By successfully coping with our challenges along the way, we seize the moment by recognizing the energy in opportunities as they arise. This is truly heroic, and each one of us can do this on any given day. Dealing with life's challenges is coping with karma. Doing our duty and evolving spiritually is our *dharma* or daily encounter with karma. Arjuna didn't curse the pressing urgency of the dawn, and neither should you.

AN INSIGHTFUL WALK ON THE BEACH

Physicist Julian Barbour took a walk with his son on the beach one bright new day. It was a special moment that he really savored. The sun shone down on them. They walked on the sand, listening to the waves that reached the shore, each in its own time. Barbour thought about time and what it meant. He looked up at the beautiful sun and considered its importance. This is when it occurred to him that the only real time in our material, mundane world is solar time. It determines everything on earth. It is the source of all energy here. All of physical life is shaped and determined by solar energy. And the moment that it strikes you is what measures time.

When this British physicist's astounding book, *The End of Time: The Next Revolution in Physics,* first appeared in the year 2000, it was met with a great deal of popular attention. Many scientists were impressed that he had tied together so many classical, conflicting views of time while seeming to advance the theory that time didn't really exist. Early reviews of his book were dazzling, but in only a few years, a few scientists began to discount Barbour's conclusion that time does not exist apart from events, the motion of the sun and stars, and the mechanical movement of a clock.

As we have seen, Barbour also noted that we randomly take notice of events in our surroundings in much the same way that a still camera takes individual frames or snapshots. We do not see everything, but only highlights that catch our attention. Barbour said we only think that we have seen every continuous motion of a gymnast who is tumbling in front of us. What we have actually seen are selected frames of the gymnast in various positions, each formed in a frozen instant. We assemble these frames like snapshots in our head and then play them forward in sequence to simulate continuous motion.

This is simply illusion, according to Barbour. To most scientists who grew up in a Newtonian universe or even a modified Newtonian universe with changes penciled in by Albert Einstein, Barbour's conclusions sound preposterous. And most of us would find it difficult to even imagine a world without time, motion, or change.

UNRELIABILITY OF HUMAN PERCEPTION

But let us investigate what Barbour calls our illusion. Let's first consider how our eyes take pictures, much like the first single-reflex cameras, which saw everything upside down. That's the way I saw the world when I first looked through the viewfinder in my training camera in Photography 101. What a single-reflex camera or any conventional photo camera sees is really light reflected off an object. The film is exposed by letting a specific amount of light through the shutter. The film is then developed. This is classical light photography, of course, although digital photography is much the same without the need for a smelly darkroom with trays of developing solution.

Our own eyes operate like the lens of a camera. We see light reflected off objects. If there is insufficient light, our eyes don't work any better than the lens of a camera in the dark. When we do see light reflected off objects, what we see is upside down and then corrected inside our brains to appear right side up. It's our own little trick photography. We process the snapshots that we have taken with our eyes inside our brains and even perform a little photo correction work to interpret how we reason the image must have looked ideally.

Even the best still photographers with the best cameras cannot catch every shot. We miss a lot. I know that's true, having worked as a photojournalist for many years. We shoot as fast as we can, but often miss moments, even when we use something like a motor drive to make the camera shoot automatically and quickly. Also, a lot of our photos are poorly shot, with bad angles, missed details, or other qualities that make them misleading as reliable documents.

It's the same with our human retinas and the way we attempt to record events in front of us with our perceptive skills. We miss a lot and don't always see things clearly. We do not see that well and take a lot of bad snapshots with our eyes. So we try to analyze what we think we have seen and rationalize what we should think of these snapshot memories of moments in our experience. This is one reason why crime scene investigators are generally confounded with conflicting accounts of eyewitnesses to the same event. They might talk to ten eyewitnesses to the same incident and get ten different stories about what really happened. Not everyone sees the same thing. People see just what they want to see. Sometimes their eyes are not wide open. Sometimes they see things from a misleading angle or with key elements not in the frame. And then, people process or interpret what they think they have seen in different ways.

We know that not everyone sees colors in the same way. So if I saw a woman with a red dress, you might see the same woman with an orange dress. And, compared with many other animals and the known range of color hues, all people have a short color range.

Defense attorneys recognize the unreliability of eyewitnesses. Professional criminals do, too, and use that as a cover to commit murder in plain daylight in a room filled with witnesses. In fact, it's in the playbook of organized crime and gangland activity, according to one tell-all book, *Joey the Hitman,* written by a former Mafia member. People who have seriously studied the gangland murders of the Prohibition era in the United States know that organized crime has long relied on unreliable eyewitnesses to confound police investigations.

We don't see well, although we like to argue in disputed discussions that *seeing is believing.* Many people believe that if they see something with their own eyes, then they can believe it happened in a certain way. We have to be realistic, however, in admitting that we don't always see things accurately, process what we've seen correctly, or catch everything. As a former reporter, I can report to you that even focused, trained observers miss things. I used to try to observe things when I would drive my little Triumph during my early newspaper days and try to determine how much I really saw of everything that passed in front of my eyes. When things got hectic, I would easily miss 80 percent of everything that passed in front of me.

You can do an experiment like this yourself. Try to keep track of everything that passes in front of you as you roll down the road in your car. Here's another exercise you can do: sit down at the end of the day and process all that you recall having seen. I would wager that you can only recall a handful of distinct images. The rest is all pretty muddled.

We have never seen anything, really, since we only see light reflected off objects. We have never seen ourselves, even in a mirror, since we are only looking at reflections of ourselves. So how can we know ourselves, if we rely on our eyes? How can we claim to know anything, based on what we have seen with our eyes? What we really see is light, or electromagnetic radiation in the form of light rays. But we usually cannot discern accurately the color of the light rays before us and so do not comprehend the special properties of the color of the light that graces us from instant to instant.

OTHER ANIMALS ARE MORE PERCEPTIVE

Cats, dogs, and other animals that live their lives in harmony with nature live in the moment, largely because they focus their attention on the energy immediately around them and the opportunity of the moment it presents. Cats can see in what we might consider darkness; they are able to realize energy even when it is dim or so faint that we perceive nothing. Consequently, they experience instants when light strikes them but is unnoticed by us. Dogs that hear a wider range of sound waves than we do probably have a better idea of time, too.

Many animals relate to electromagnetic radiation better than people, who do not live as close to nature with the same level of perceptive awareness and harmonic resonance. They know when a storm is coming and when other danger approaches. They know when the sun sets that it is the time to retreat and when the sun rises it is the time to seize the moment. Every day holds new opportunity for those who are aware. Carlos Castaneda described a cat's awareness and ability to seize the moment to save its skin in an instant of looming danger as a cat's "cubic centimeter of chance." He said that a cat seems to sense when you are taking it to the veterinarian or about to euthanize it. Dogs, cats, and other critters that live close to nature have a perceptive awareness that we have often dismissed as "animal instinct." Maybe a better way of describing this animal cunning is "living fully in the moment with conscious awareness."

STRIKING GOLD

We encounter different opportunities from moment to moment, if we are alert. Sometimes, however, people get fixated on the same opportunity, with eyes closed to all the new opportunities that are daily coming our way. When one or two prospectors struck gold in California in the mid-1800s, many people headed to the site with the belief there would be gold for everyone. Opportunity doesn't work that way, of course. Your opportunity will likely be a little different from mine, even if we are in the same place and time.

Would-be prospectors left their homes and loved ones to head to California in droves, plodding their way with rickety wagons pulled by tired oxen and horses. No sacrifice was too big to get to the promised land. Only a relative few of them actually found significant amounts of gold, however. They felt that gold was just downstream or just upstream from where their sifting pans came up empty.

A few clever people who were drawn to California adapted to new opportunities along the way. Some found suitable farmland nearby. Others became ranchers in new settlements. The new West was lush, green, and filled with potential. Trees were everywhere. The water was pure. The land was available to start a bold, new life. Some enterprising people in the gold rush saw a new opportunity in the sale of merchandise to the many would-be prospectors.

When the gold played out, many people with glitter still in their eyes looked elsewhere for free gold. They trekked to Alaska to seek their fortune. A few people found gold, of course, but many others died along the arduous journey in the vast expanses of snow and ice. But Alaska held many opportunities for those whose eyes were open wide with focused attention to the power of the moment. Alaska, or the Great Land, as Native peoples called it, held many resources. Many early travelers to Alaska became fishermen, loggers, storekeepers, and farmers. It was a great place to homestead, with enough land for everyone.

Once the gold strikes of Alaska, California, and other places played out, gold fever ended. There was a limit to the gold. It was no longer easy to find. So even the prospectors who found a little gold eventually called it quits. Gold strikes don't last long, and they don't enrich that many people. Some old sourdough prospectors stayed too long at their claims, looking for gold long after the gold rush ended. Second strikes at the same site are rare. Opportunities come, and opportunities go. They will last just an instant. The next instant brings another kind of opportunity.

LIGHTNING STRIKES TWICE

It is possible to attract the right kind of energy to you at just the right moment. Consider lightning and where it strikes. Popular folklore suggests that lightning doesn't strike twice in the same place. On the other hand, lightning can be attracted to a lightning rod. Big buildings often have one, towering high above the city. Consider how you can attract energy to you, too. You can become a lightning rod. It's a matter of attracting the right kind of karma.

Remember that karma is personal opportunity and it operates as a natural force in the universe. Like everything else in manifest creation, it is subjected to the radiant electromagnetic energy that is present everywhere around you. If you have enough personal awareness and focus your consciousness on it, you can draw karma to you. What karma you attract, of course, depends on you and your right actions. According to Krishnamurti, like right action, right thought also can direct energy to you; both will affect your karma. When you attract karma, you attract energy and opportunity. The real trick to life mastery, perhaps, is recognizing opportunity when it comes your way, knowing how to handle it, and knowing how to put it to good use. That's the real hero's journey—learning to seize the moment.

VISUALIZATION IN ACTIVE, FOCUSED MEDITATION

The type of meditation we propose in this practical guide is different from most mediation. Our approach to meditation is patterned after that of the Western shamanic spirit walkers or dream walkers and Hindu *samadhi* mystics. *Samadhi,* a Sanskrit word from ancient Indian philosophy, describes advanced yogic schools in Hinduism and Buddhism that train people in the highest spiritual levels of concentrated meditation. Samadhi mystics go into deep meditative states to leave the body, traveling outside normal time and space. There are three basic things that are different about their meditative states:

1. These are *active* meditations that require a lot of focus.
2. They incorporate *visualization* where you create with thought power the intent of what you want to do and where you want to go in your active meditation.
3. They are out-of-body experiences.

We can practice these three basic components in a visualization exercise.

VISUALIZATION EXERCISE

Any effective visualization always has two basic parts. The first part is what you create in your mind's eye as a picture. This should be created with as much detail as possible. The second part is to visualize what you have created in your mind's eye as already taking place. This gives it life. Many people forget the second part, which is the real magic of creation—giving it life. Without this component, your creative visualization is simply an idle wish you have dreamed.

What You Need

- A quiet, secluded room where you can meditate.
- Loose-fitting clothing, with your shoes removed.
- A mat, blanket, or pad on which to recline on your back on the ground. (This exercise can also be done sitting in a straight-backed chair with your feet firmly on the ground, arms and feet uncrossed, and erect posture, although results will probably be better if you recline on your back.)

Procedure

1. Lie on your back on the ground (or sit in a chair) with arms and legs uncrossed, so that energy flows freely through your body.
2. Begin deep, controlled breathing and allow your body to become numb as you focus on a still, quiet point deep within you where spirit resides.
3. Clear your mind and tune out all external and internal distractions until you see a blank slate in your mind's eye. Focus on this slate.
4. Slowly begin to visualize your intent in the coming out-of-body part of the meditation, picturing first what you want to do and then where you want to go. In this part of the meditation you need to visualize leaving the body when you reach a deep meditative state, where you will go, and what you will do when you get there. Do not think in terms of words or concepts, but only visualize your intent as a picture in your mind's eye.
5. Remember that words, thoughts, and analysis hamper good meditation. These are functions of the lower, rational mind. Learn to visualize. Without analyzing what you have visualized, simply tuck these pictures away to carry with you into the next part of your meditation, where they will be released like a posthypnotic suggestion to yourself.
6. Once you are satisfied with your creative visualization, begin the second part of your meditation with the understanding that the pictures you have carefully crafted in your mind's eye will be carried gently with you into your new consciousness state and brought forward when you are ready to leave your body. Implementation of your creative visualizations as a road map in your out-of-body meditation will be automatic.

SEEING WITH NEW EYES AND HEARING WITH NEW EARS

What You Need

- A noisy room with people all around you.
- An adjacent room with more people talking earnestly to each other outside your normal range of hearing.
- A chair for you to sit in a place where you will not be bumped, jostled, or engaged by people in your room. (The chair is optional, as you could also stand.)
- Loose-fitting clothing that will not constrain you in any way. (You might also loosen or even remove your shoes, if that is possible without drawing unwanted attention to yourself.)

Procedure

1. Go into a meditation, tuning out all of the noise and distractions immediately around you. You need to filter out the distractions.
2. Tune out all internal chatter and thought, so that you are not thinking of anything.
3. Keep your feet firmly on the ground and your posture erect without bodily movement. Consciously put your body to sleep, so that you have no feeling in your hands, feet, arms, or legs.
4. Go deep within yourself to the center of your being where spirit resides and begin controlled breathing.
5. Observe that your higher consciousness is keenly alert while your physical body rests.
6. Focus your conscious awareness on conversations in the outer room to hear what is being said in the room outside where you are stationed. To do this, you must continue to tune out immediate distractions and filter only what you observe in the next room.

Recapitulation

- Were you able to pick up on conversations in the next room? If so, check with people in the next room to see if your observations were accurate. If you do not know the people in the next room well enough to ask them directly, you might linger in the next room to determine whether the voices you heard are present there and the conversations you heard from afar seem to fit what you hear while in the same room.

- When you observed what was being said in the next room, were you also able to see the people in your mind's eye?
- Does it now seem plausible to you that your consciousness actually left your body to visit the next room?
- If you were successful in this exercise, next try observing people and their conversations outside the building where you are stationed. If you were unsuccessful, repeat the exercise with greater focus to meditate and leave your body with your consciousness.

4

Fourth Secret of Time

TIMELESSNESS: BEYOND TIME AS WE KNOW IT

We experience a sense of timelessness during deep meditations, as we have seen. You might say, then, that meditation is a way to escape time or eclipse time. In this meditative state of timelessness, we can go places and do things in a flash that would ordinarily take us hours or even days in the physical world. The explanation for this is simple. Our consciousness as energy waves travels at the speed of light (one billion feet per second) and possibly faster.

Think about how fast your thoughts travel. It's pretty instantaneous, isn't it? You can send your thoughts to someone halfway across the world at a certain instant and later verify that your loved one received your thoughts just about the same time that you sent them. People who are closely connected have sensed loved ones dying just at the moment of death or sensed their danger half a world away. Have you ever thought of somebody just at the instant this person called you, seeming to know in advance that your phone was going to ring?

We are connected to our loved ones by our thoughts. Our thoughts are energy waves of our consciousness.

THE AMAZING SPEED AND ENERGY OF CONSCIOUSNESS

Some of the first modern descriptions of consciousness outside the body were Theosophical discussions. The first significant book, perhaps, was Theosophist Annie Besant's *Thought Power*. Our thoughts, she determined, are not held secretly inside our heads, but are actually dispatched—either on purpose or else accidentally. She considered how our thoughts can be demonstrated to leave our body and be directed in specific ways as invisible arrows that reach their target with pinpoint precision and great impact. This groundbreaking book was followed in 1901 by *Thought-Forms* by Besant and clairvoyant healer Charles W. Leadbeater. In this book, Besant and Leadbeater describe how our thoughts have a radiating vibration as energy and can also be seen as floating, patterned forms that are visible to clairvoyants. Furthermore, our conscious thoughts outside the body can be seen in various colors and shapes that are influenced and altered by music, color, and emotions. After all, music is vibrating wave energy, just as light is vibrating wave energy, and our emotions create emotional energy. The notes of music, colors of light, and types of emotions influence the nature of our thought-forms. As we dispatch our thoughts from our body, they impact other people intentionally or even unintentionally, as with wild thoughts gone astray. Our thoughts can heal or cause damage like a loaded gun. Consequently, in terms of personal responsibility and karma, we are accountable for their impact as energy outbursts.

At the time of these early books on thought-forms, the only way to verify their claims that thoughts possess power and form outside the body was through clairvoyant observation. More recently, the well-documented and often-replicated experiments of Masaru Emoto, described in his book *The Miracle of Water,* show how thoughts that are verbalized aloud or written down can be transported over distances with amazing effects, bringing about sudden healing and change. Our life-force energy resonates with others over great distances. In some of his experiments, Dr. Emoto used the words *love* and *gratitude* to alter water, leading it to form elaborate crystals. In another experiment, children were asked to write a word on a piece of paper in a distance-healing exercise. The photographed results of the many people who were involved in these successful experiments around the world offer proof that our thoughts are easily transported with a natural vibration to bring about instantaneous changes. In addition to Dr. Emoto's book, his experiments can be viewed in a DVD documentary of the same title. His experiments are also featured in the popular film *What the Bleep Do We Know,* along with cutting-edge scientific observations from nuclear physicist and Professor Emeritus William Tiller, Ph.D.

Medical science, of course, traditionally discounts the effects of good thoughts, prayers, or meditations that are employed to assist other people to heal. It tends to believe that you can convince yourself to heal, however, with the confidence that your prayers for yourself will make you better. It just doesn't believe that your prayers, meditations, or loving thoughts exist outside your personal feelings about yourself or that they go anywhere outside you.

We might add that medical science does not much believe in consciousness. Medical science tends to believe only in the material world, the concrete world of things it sees or thinks it sees. It believes in the almighty power of the human brain and discounts the possibility that anything carries thought beyond the physical cranium that sits atop your shoulders. It believes—or claims to believe—only in science and the scientific approach, knowing full well that the scientific approach is flawed by the presence of the observer, who is biased in attempts to prove a preconceived notion. We might add that medical doctors are a very confused lot from the day they leave school, clutching a degree in arts with the belief that they are scientists. As medical doctors, they are really poised to enter the healing arts. But they don't understand that healing is an art and not something that can be simply measured out in chemical compounds. Hence, medical science is not objective and believes only in the material world—a very restricted, reductionist outlook.

DOCUMENTING CONSCIOUSNESS BEYOND THE BODY

The very idea that ten people could meditate together to bring peace or major change to the world might seem somewhat preposterous to people of medical science. The claim that Ian Fleming, Sybil Leek, and others helped the Allies defeat the Axis powers during World War II by silently gathering is impossible for them to grasp. The work of people with Maria Montessori to bring about peace through peace meditations must seem like fantasy to scientists who do not believe in consciousness, let alone the power of consciousness to bring about change. How could they believe that only ten people who practice Transcendental Meditation together could have any sort of real impact on the world around them? They simply cannot accept that our conscious thoughts can exist outside the physical body.

Yet people who have died for a few minutes and returned to life report conscious thoughts outside the physical body. It is rather obvious from the great amount of documented cases in near-death experiences that consciousness is not limited by any condition of the physical body. Brad Steiger's amazing book *One with the Light* is just one example of documented research that proves consciousness operates at a high level outside the physical body. If our consciousness is pure energy and represents our life force or spirit, how can it die with the expiration of the human body?

Clinical research into remembered past lives through hypnotic past-life regression also shows that consciousness extends beyond the physical body and carries forward from life to life. The groundbreaking work of Ian Stevenson with his books *Twenty Cases Suggestive of Reincarnation* and *Children Who Remember Previous Lives* helped spark a whole new, serious investigation into evidence of past lives. This careful research is continuing under serious scholars such as Tom Shroder, who wrote *Old Souls: Compelling Evidence from Children Who Remember Past Lives.* Curious skeptics might be interested to know that many people who remember past lives have been interviewed in documentaries that are readily available for home viewing, such as *In Another Life: Reincarnation in America,* a DVD that features firsthand accounts of people in interviews with researchers from many years of careful study.

CONSCIOUSNESS IN OUR DREAMS

As energy, our consciousness travels with grace and power beyond any limitations of time or space. It travels freely in our dreams every night. The proof that our consciousness leaves our sleeping bodies during dreams is evident in the fact that people routinely experience a sense of timelessness in dream situations. Think back yourself to some of your own recent dreams and reflect on all that happens in just a few clicks of the clock in your bedroom. Our consciousness in dreams is not restricted by limitations of the physical world. There is no physical sense of time or space in our dreams when we fly outside our bodies, visit places far away, experience a long series of events, and travel freely to the past and the future to live a life outside our physical reality.

We also have some very mundane dreams, of course, where the brain is simply mulling over concerns of the past or anxiety about the future. These are repetitive dreams, often viewed as anxiety nightmares. But many of our dreams take us outside our physical prisons. In the dream state our consciousness can take us almost anywhere to do almost anything. In this state, the rules of the physical universe and our physical senses do not apply. In the exotic realm of our dreams, we can smell the color blue and taste the morning light. Our consciousness allows us to experience an expanded reality with new awareness, all in the twinkling of an eye. Have you ever dreamed half of a lifetime in one short night?

Have you ever traveled beyond the known world or visited moments in your past during one brief dream?

We must learn to treat our dreams as a learning experience, as our consciousness longs to explore and grow when freed from the constraints of physical encasement. People who record their experiences upon first waking and then meditate on the dream experience often find that they can begin to understand where they go in their dreams and what these exotic encounters mean. Only your consciousness knows where you have been in your dreams. Meditation on your dreams, therefore, allows your consciousness to sort it out for you, as only you can do in a state of higher consciousness.

Many people, sadly, are unable to acknowledge their amazing journeys outside space and time in their dream states. This is because their physical bodies and analytical brains are unable to recognize their spirit bodies and higher consciousness. To them, it is preposterous that their spirit could soar freely on the wings of a higher consciousness that can exist outside the physical body. The physical side of us and that little pocket calculator that likes to call itself our brain is uncomfortable with the idea of another force within us that is not material and within its control.

In India, where meditation has long been accepted, people do not experience this discomfort with the release of consciousness during dreams. In fact, conscious dreaming is an early level of samadhi mystic training.* The samadhi novice does not immediately attempt deep, waking meditation to enter a state of timelessness. A very early level of samadhi training involves exercises in controlled dream travel. In these exercises, the mystic practices leaving the physical body during dreams to travel in a pure consciousness body as energy leaving the physical realm.

To benefit from dream travel, however, a person must be able to

---

*Students in this yogic tradition go through many levels of training in the East. This form of deep meditation is seldom taught in the West, although there are now a few samadhi training centers in North America, including ones in Denver, Colorado, and Newton, Massachusetts.

recognize these exotic dreams outside space and time. Many people who are unable to do this will simply say that they don't dream anything memorable or even remember dreaming at all. It's just easier for them on a physical level to deny the whole experience and take no note of it whatsoever.

STOPPING THE WORLD

Many people who deny traveling in their dreams also deny the evidence of remembered past lives and discount near-death experiences as well. Their first recognized experience with consciousness outside the body during active meditation, then, might be viewed as a physically rewarding experience, as their body learns to relax and release control. As they get into a more serious study and application of meditation, they can experience on a deeper level what it means to stop time and experience timelessness by going outside the physical body.

"Stop the world," was the advice of author Carlos Castaneda in his amazing book *Journey to Ixtlan,* based on Yaqui shamanism of Mexico. This is not to say that we stop the rain, winds, or the forces around us. We can simply stop our own involvement with the physical world around us and the spinning web of confusion and noise that fights for our constant attention. We can change our perception of all of this during meditation. We can tune out the outer din and reach inner peace deep within ourselves where spirit resides. We can put our analytical brain into a sleeping mode and engage the super computer that is our higher consciousness.

Stopping the world to enter a meditation state of blissful peace and out-of-body timelessness is not easy for many of us. Many people find it difficult to tune out external distractions. To do this, you must control your physical senses. We can tell ourselves not to be distracted by the fragrances, compelling images, and startling sounds that compete for our attention. We do this not to be dead to the beauty and majesty of the physical world around us, but to focus on attaining another higher level of consciousness without distractions. The beauty and aroma of a daffodil or perfume can be overpowering. The chatter of children can be either amusing or bothersome, but always hard to ignore. Consider that we are not turning our backs on the world around us, but taking a little break from all of the hubbub to explore higher consciousness beyond this limited reality.

Maurice Merleau-Ponty, the early-twentieth-century author of *Phenomenology of Perception,* was one of the first people to write about the role of perception in how we shape our world. He suggested that we can selectively shut down sensory awareness of the immediate, physical world around us. The mystic does this to leave the ordinary world and enter a nonordinary reality. The brain no longer processes the physical senses of smell, touch, hearing, or seeing in the ordinary way. It is much the same as being asleep and not alert to the sounds and smells in the room where you recline. The ordinary world is like a blender that gets you all caught up inside its spinning confusion. It grinds you up and spits you out in its own image. You must learn to control your perceptive awareness if you want to seize the moment and experience something much more profound beyond this world.

If you really think about it, you will realize that you already have the ability to tune out distractions and selectively focus to reach a different level of consciousness. You might have experienced this as a school child on the baseball field when you tuned out all distractions when it came your turn to bat. Perhaps you can recall making the fastball headed your way slow down in your mind's eye. Top athletes often describe this sensation of slowing things down as "being in the zone." The best batters do this. Other athletes do, too, according to accounts of top performers in the book *The Sweet Spot in Time* by John Jerome. This is creating timelessness or stopping time.

Or perhaps you have found yourself in a crowded, noisy room where you were able to tune out most of the clamoring noise to hear only one voice in the crowd. I experienced this in a dining room in Oregon during a Chamber of Commerce dinner. I found that I could tune out all of the clamor to hear just one voice. I discovered that in a state of

heightened consciousness I could focus my attention and make everything appear to move in slow motion. If I released my focused attention
even a little, the sounds would return and the motion of activity would
appear to speed up again. It was an eerie experience, but one that it is
possible for you to replicate. If you do it right, you should be able to
meditate in a crowd or even with blaring horns and sirens all around
you. You can learn to meditate with your eyes wide open or your eyes
shut. With practice, you can meditate anywhere and reach higher consciousness states quickly. This is simply selective perception or controlling your sensory overload. This is stopping the world.

Once you have learned to enter this state of higher consciousness,
you will be able to enter a state of timelessness, where almost anything
you can imagine will be possible for you to experience. Zen masters and
warrior athletes do this all of the time. Dan Millman, a former world
champion athlete, wrote about his martial-arts approach to entering
higher states of conscious awareness in his groundbreaking book *The
Warrior Athlete,* later reissued as *The Inner Athlete.*

The first thing you must do to stop the world is gain control over
your physical body and reach a place of inner peace and quiet. With
practice, anyone can learn to do this. An exercise at the end of this
chapter will help you. Once you experience this state, you will be able
to return to it freely. Your spirit longs to be free and seeks release, if you
will provide it.

APPROACHING THE SPEED OF LIGHT

When we learn to enter a state of deep meditation in which our higher
consciousness leaves our physical body, we suspend time and escape the
limitation of space. We can go almost anywhere, including places outside the physical world as we commonly know it. That shouldn't surprise you when you consider that your consciousness as energy is not
bound by the physical limitations of this earth plane once it leaves the
boundaries of your body.

However, in meditative states most people visit places they know very well. They visit physical locations on the earth and in their own time frame. That is not to say that we cannot visit exotic universes and alternate realities beyond the mundane physical world or situations in the past or future. We simply elect to go places where we are comfortable or where we have a great sense of personal attachment. These are normally places known to us in our current, everyday life.

In a state of heightened awareness outside the body, the normal flow of time appears to slow down until it stands still. Freed from the physical body and the socially induced perception of time moving forward, our consciousness experiences many things as happening "now," with no loss of time. Nothing outside the physical world is fixed and rigid without wiggle room. The world outside our physical restrictions is ever expanding with infinite possibilities. And everything is happening now. Where we choose to go and what we choose to do when our consciousness leaves our body is up to us. There is no other force that guides us. Our spirit longs to be free to explore, grow, and evolve spiritually in our understanding of who we are and the nature of creation.

There are many mysteries. You can take your own journey to find your own answers. You can be your own guide and guardian, your own teacher and also the student. Once your spirit leaves your physical body in pure conscious energy, it is free to roam unrestricted. You can do an infinite amount of exploring as a spiritual traveler outside the body. Hopefully, your journeys will take you to understanding of the significant questions that confront us, beyond the petty concerns of our physical life as little, insecure egos.

It is true, however, that many novices or untrained people who attempt to meditate will never experience timelessness or a spiritual journey that leads to any significant answers of real concern. These are people who have never allowed their consciousness to leave their physical body and do this sort of soul travel. Stories of astral travel seem alien to them. They simply cannot accept the large body of testimony and observation that consciousness can leave the physical body and roam anywhere and any time with totally unrestricted freedom. In astral travel, the consciousness and subtle energy body of a person in deep meditation leave the physical body. Consciousness is not restricted to the physical body as a part of the human brain, but can exist out of body as spirit energy in a subtle astral body. The very idea of thought-forms leaving the body, however, seems questionable to many They do not even trust their dreams and dismiss them as fancy. They doubt stories of near-death encounters where people have powerful encounters, with their consciousness hovering outside their limp bodies. They don't have enough real proof of reincarnation to satisfy them that consciousness survives its physical host body. They are afraid to really meditate and leave their bodies.

Or perhaps they are simply afraid to release their inner life force and float unfettered, without all the weight and safe enclosure of a physical form that is firmly anchored on the ground. Perhaps they fear they might leave their bodies and not know where to go, how to get there, and how to get back safely. It takes courage to begin a hero's quest, to step into darkness, not always knowing where the unmarked trail might lead. That's what discovery is all about.

We can only experience timelessness and stop the world when we step outside our physical bodies and escape the limitations of time and space that make this material world a restricted zone. When we do this consciously, with focus, we literally become free spirits. On this journey of discovery, our free spirits can soar freely into the past or into the future, exploring a flexible time line where every time and every thing is readily available. There is no fixed time outside the manifest world of our fixed, restricted existence as corporeal beings. There are no boundaries or limited dimensions in the unmanifest world. There are no limitations arising from our restricted capacities for smelling, touching, feeling, hearing, or sensing. Nothing is fixed. Everything is filled with potential, waiting for change and waiting to be discovered. And time is elastic.

We do not create timelessness. We discover it. Timelessness is the normal state of being outside our little, physical existence. If we leave our small-minded, linear thinking behind and consider that time does not flow forward in a straight line but might be something entirely different and not measured physically, then we realize how our spiritual journeys outside our physical bodies can take us anywhere at any time we care to venture.

I have selected some tried and true exercises in consciousness training to help you experience these points, so that you will feel comfortable in leaving your body outside time and space.

STOPPING THE WORLD

What You Need

- An enclosed room where you will be uninterrupted.
- Some recorded music that you can turn on and let play.
- A straight-backed chair to sit on.
- Loose-fitting clothing.

Procedure

1. Close the door.
2. Turn on the music so that it's very audible to you.
3. Sit in the chair with erect posture and feet firmly grounded.
4. With eyes open, enter a state of heightened consciousness with focused awareness. Begin deep, controlled breathing.
5. Tune out all distractions and internal thought, focusing only on the sound of the music.
6. With your focused concentration, make the music begin to fade.
7. Continue fading out the sound until you hear no music.

STOPPING THE WORLD VARIATION 1

What You Need

- An enclosed room where you will be uninterrupted.
- A person who will be facing you and speaking to you directly.
- A straight-backed chair for you to sit on.
- Loose-fitting clothing.

Procedure

1. Close the door.
2. Sit in your chair with erect posture and feet firmly grounded.
3. Have the person who is to speak face you and begin to speak.
4. With eyes open, enter a state of heightened consciousness with focused awareness. Begin deep, controlled breathing.
5. Tune out all distractions and internal thought, focusing only on the sound of the person who is speaking to you.
6. With your focused concentration, make the sound of the speaker's voice begin to fade out. Make certain that you watch the lips of the speaker.
7. Continue to fade out the sound until you hear nothing but silence.

STOPPING THE WORLD VARIATION 2

What You Need

- An enclosed room where you will be uninterrupted.
- A sound recording or person to speak directly to you.
- A straight-backed chair for you to sit on.
- Loose-fitting clothing.

Procedure

1. Close the door.
2. Start the music or have the person you have selected begin to speak.
3. Sit in your chair with erect posture and feet firmly grounded.
4. With eyes open, enter a state of heightened consciousness with focused awareness. Begin deep, controlled breathing.
5. Tune out all distractions and internal thought, focusing only on the sound.
6. Face the sound and stare at it.
7. With your focused concentration, make the sound begin to fade.
8. Now with your focused concentration, allow the sound to become audibly louder.
9. Now use your focused concentration to make the sound fade out entirely.
10. Slowly restore the sound, little by little.

Recapitulation

- If you had trouble manipulating your sensory perception and controlling the level of the sound, try the exercise again after first visualizing your will center in your lower abdomen and gaining a feeling of the power of your will that emanates from this region when summoned to give you power.
- It is important that you enter a meditative state with eyes wide open in the Buddhist way, so that you are consciously aware of the things in the room.
- Do not be discouraged if you are unable to control the sound and stop the world at first. This exercise, like all of the exercises in this book, is designed to give you a feeling for how to control the world around you to gain freedom. It takes practice. Moreover, it requires that you get a feel for how this is done on all levels of your being.

FADE TO BLACK

What You Need

- A solid, straight-backed chair.
- A quiet, dimly lit room.
- Loose-fitting clothing.

Procedure

1. Sit in the chair with erect posture and feet firmly grounded.
2. Do not cross your hands or feet, but allow energy to flow freely in your body.
3. Visualize that you will see a blank slate in your mind's eye when you enter a state of higher consciousness and then tuck that picture away to retrieve later.
4. Close your eyes and meditate, tuning out all external and internal distractions.
5. As your physical body becomes numb, your higher consciousness begins to accelerate. Begin deep, controlled breathing.
6. When you feel that you have cleared yourself of all internal thoughts and outer distractions, picture the blank slate in your mind's eye like a blackboard with nothing yet written on it. Focus on this blackboard.

FADE TO BLACK VARIATION

Procedure

1. As before, sit in the chair with erect posture and feet firmly grounded.

2. Do not cross your hands or feet, but allow energy to flow freely in your body.

3. Visualize that you are going to see black in your mind's eye when you enter a state of higher consciousness and then tuck that picture away to retrieve later. Envision it as a thick field of blackness that will be all around you.

4. Now visualize that when you enter the blackness, you will allow yourself to be whisked away from the room where you sit into the great unknown in a controlled out-of-body experience for spiritual exploration.

5. Close your eyes and meditate, tuning out all external and internal distractions.

6. As your physical body becomes numb, your higher consciousness begins to accelerate.

7. When you feel that you have cleared yourself of all internal thought and outer distractions, bring forward your stored visualization of blackness as a manifestation.

8. When you experience the blackness engulfing you, bring forward your visualization to allow yourself to be whisked away. Your inner life force will leave your body to enter the great blackness of the unknown on a controlled journey of spiritual discovery.

9. Gently return to your body whenever you like by simply thinking of your physical self resting in the chair.

Recapitulation

- Out of darkness, all things come. The darkness is the great expanse that is yet to be discovered. It is the place where new life is formed. It holds the answers to your questions. Once we enter the darkness with our life force, we find illumination and have no difficulty seeing. You might think of the blackness as a barrier that you pass through initially as you become accustomed to leaving your body. Beyond this barrier you will find light.

- If you experienced difficulty in seeing the blackness in your mind's eye or entering the black expanse, it is probably because you are reluctant to let yourself go. Remember that your spirit longs to be free. Spend some additional time in inner dialogue, assuring your physical self that there is no danger in allowing your consciousness to leave the body in a safe, controlled setting and that the body left behind will be rewarded with peaceful rest during the absence of your higher consciousness.

VISIT YOUR OWN SPECIAL HEALING PLACE

What You Need

- A quiet, enclosed room for meditation.
- A mat, pad, or blanket on which to recline on your back.
- Loose-fitting clothing, with your shoes removed.

Procedure

1. Lie on your back with arms and legs extended and eyes open.
2. Visualize in your mind's eye visiting a place of personal safety and healing that is your ideal power spot and place to revitalize yourself. It might be a place on this earth that is dear to you or an idealized place. Maybe it's a place in the woods, a place by the water, or a place on a hillside. Then again, maybe it's a place outside this physical world, created by your own imagination. Picture it in your mind's eye, even though the whole scene might not appear to you at first in minute detail.
3. Close your eyes and enter a state of meditation, tuning out all external and internal distractions. Begin deep, controlled breathing.
4. When you sense that you have reached that still, quiet place deep within you where spirit resides, then bring your visualization before your mind's eye without thoughts or words. Simply look at the picture that you have created and bought with you into meditation. You should instantly find yourself transported to that place.
5. When you arrive in your special power place, look around you to take in the details of the scene. Perhaps you will observe a colored light that surrounds you with healing energy. Feel the power.

6. You feel safe and secure in this place. You are protected here and alone. Let the healing energy of this special place engulf you and run through you, healing and revitalizing you. Feel the warmth of the energy as it enters you and strengthens you.

7. When you feel energized, gently return to your physical body back in the room by simply thinking about returning to your body. This will be effortless, as you are attached, despite the separation.

8. After you have returned your consciousness to your body and feel sensations in your body once again, slowly open your eyes and carefully rise to your feet.

Recapitulation

• This is my favorite meditation. Anyone can build such a place for personal use. It provides you with a personal power spot that you can visit any time when you sense a need to heal, reenergize, seek comfort, or find security and protection for yourself. It is your special place that you have created just for yourself.

• As you become accustomed to visiting this place, you will find it increasingly easy to return there whenever needed, with little or no effort. You will find that your spirit rushes back to this place, even if you are standing or sitting without much preparation for meditation.

• You will naturally find the colors of healing light energy that you need there, as your spirit instinctively knows what you need. You will find yourself blanketed by this healing light.

• Some people might hear healing music there.

• In time, you will be able to visit this special healing place with all of your subtle energy bodies (described in the next chapter). This will happen all on its own, as spirit becomes comfortable with the journey.

Fifth Secret of Time

TRAVERSING TIME
AND MERGING TIME LINES

Our physical brain jealously guards its domain, which it considers to be everything that it can claim. It makes its claim in much the way mining claims were recorded and credited during the gold rush years. It weighs and measures, then analyzes things. It likes to size up things and considers itself good at being the best and ultimate arbitrator.

Human beings, as problem-solving primates with nice clothes, value their brains and ability to reason. We value our brains so much, in fact, that we let them rule our lives. After all, we proudly possess the ability to reason. How we reason, however, is another story.

We like to keep tabs on everything and maintain control by determining how things measure up. That goes with anything. We measure our houses, our distance to work, our income, our shoe size and ring size, our children's height and weight, our car engines, and the number of steps we need to take in all critical situations. A critical situation can be anything from how far we need to walk up to our apartment to how many steps we will need to take to deal with a major problem in our life. To the analytical brain with its little corner on control, everything becomes a physical measurement.

Many people take comfort, then, in having the trusty tools to measure the world around them. They proudly wield their tape measures and their marking pens. They record their future challenges on calendars and in scheduling books. If something can't be easily sized up, they "stick a pin in it" to mark the spot. Even that gives them some small measure of assurance.

Our physical surroundings might be restrictive, but we somehow find comfort in saying that our bed is standard size, our home is split level, or the cell in which we are imprisoned every night measures eight feet by eight feet with plenty of headroom.

We even attempt to measure time. In fact, measuring accomplishments against how long they appear to take in terms of time seems to provide a special measure of satisfaction for well-dressed primates with toolboxes. The best among us can boast the ability to run a four-minute mile or a hundred-yard dash in eight seconds flat. We impose deadlines to measure how much we can accomplish in a set amount of time.

Sadly, however, there is little real change as a result of all of this measuring. We see a runner beginning a race at the starting block and take a mental snapshot of that instant. Then we watch the runner beginning to move forward and make more mental snapshots with our upside-down, selective way of seeing reflected light. In truth, we never do see the runner, but only the light reflected off the runner at various instants that we record in our minds. We see the runner finishing the race at the same instant that a stopwatch has measured a certain number of clicks on its dial. To make this little story seem continuous, progressive, and positive, we say that our hero has run a four-minute mile. That is based on our poor vision as it selectively records various instants when light strikes an object here and there. Then inside our brains, we make a movie out of what we would prefer to believe we have observed:

continuous action measured by time moving forward progressively.

This is all based on our relative perception. Our ability to perceive, as Ouspensky and Merleau-Ponty have outlined, is severely limited by our senses and our three-dimensional approach to reality in this physical world. Perhaps the Greek philosopher Plato said it best in his allegory of the cave. It is hard to perceive true reality with our eyes when we are trapped in a cave and looking at shadows dancing in the distance. Perhaps we are all like these cave dwellers in trying to determine what we think we see in the distant light. Even when we try to improve our measuring skills with something like binoculars, we are only looking through a glass darkly and forming subjective opinions about what we believe to be reality.

Ouspensky, like Plato, believed that our vantage point impairs our perceptive skills. Ouspensky, however, felt that the problem is much more than whether we are standing in a dark cave and looking at a wall. Every place in this physical world, according to Ouspensky in *Tertium Organum,* is restricted. We live in a flat, three-dimensional world. Above our three-dimensional world could be a four-dimensional world with people who can readily perceive four dimensions. Below us could be another world of fewer dimensions. But our physical world has its limitations. Ouspensky hinted that we might advance beyond a three-dimensional reality, but only with higher consciousness to take us outside our physical boundaries.

Once out of the body, our human consciousness can experience timelessness. This journey of discovery takes us beyond the limitations of mundane space and time as we commonly know them. Advanced samadhi mystics in India go into deep meditation trances during their soul travels beyond time and space. They are sometimes gone from their bodies for a couple of days, as measured by people in the physical universe. In fact, many samadhi mystics in this deep meditative state were picked up and successfully moved during a recent tsunami storm that wreaked havoc in India and south of India.

IS PHYSICAL TIME TRAVEL POSSIBLE?

Beyond consciousness and the projection of energy bodies, is physical time travel possible? Einstein seemed to think that it is. The young Albert Einstein was influenced by the science fiction model of H. G. Wells's 1895 classic, *The Time Machine*. In that book the hero, a scientist, builds a time machine that he can ride into the past or future. It disappears before the very eyes of people in the physical here and now in a flash of light and reappears in another time period.

Einstein was an imaginative physicist who stared up at the sky after much reflection and was inspired by the light that he saw. According to him, uniform or universal time does not exist. Time exists only as the measured lapse between two events. Experiencing time in this fashion varies from one observer to another, dependent on the relative speed of the observer's reference frames, which he calls space and time locations or space-time. He refers to various "instants" or slices of earth time as the point at which electromagnetic radiation (light) strikes an individual object or being, each in turn. We might consider this instant as Now. Light strikes an individual in New Delhi at a different instant than when it strikes an individual in London. Hence, we determine time by when light strikes us. Furthermore, light bends when traveling around the sun or other astronomical bodies, allowing for curves in space-time. Light that travels from our world and our galaxy outward across the universe will eventually return in a complete round-trip of the universe!

Einstein saw light and the speed of light as the one universal, uniform law of the universe. He said that there was a speed limit in our universe, the speed of light, which travels at one billion feet per second. He said in his special theory of relativity that a clock will slow down as it moves through space faster and faster and approaches the speed of light. Upon reaching the speed of light, a clock would stop entirely and the perception of time would dissolve. In theory, we also could escape the restraints of fixed time as we know it by exceeding the speed of light.

Theoretically, then, Albert Einstein proposed that time travel is possible. Einstein's idea of how to exceed the speed of light, however, involved finding black holes in space and traveling through them, something that nobody has done yet. He also suggested that mass that exceeds the speed of light would reach infinity and disappear, transforming into energy. Energy can travel freely at such speeds, while physical mass cannot. People as physical beings are mass. Physical bodies cannot exceed the speed of light and remain physical bodies. How, then, can we ever exceed the speed of light?

Atomic particle separator labs are searching for hidden possibilities. These are huge, extremely expensive facilities without any real practical experience or answers yet. Nonetheless, people like astrophysicist J. Richard Gott of Princeton, author of the wonderful book *Time Travel in Einstein's Universe: The Physical Possibilities of Travel through Time*, believe that atomic particle separator labs might one day produce a real, working time machine.

Of course, this is theoretical science. Will super colliders give us working physical models or information about the energy within the atom? Super colliders seek to smash together subatomic particles at incredible force and along the way unlock new dimensions of space-time. Such a massive particle accelerator is theoretically capable of reproducing energies present at the big bang of initial creation. We naturally wonder, however, whether that will allow our physical bodies to travel at the speed of light or faster.

Professor Gott, a distinguished and inspiring scientist, suggests that we have all experienced time travel already by simply standing in front of a mirror and realizing that the light struck the mirror at a different time than when it struck us. This seems like an odd way to determine reality, however, when you consider how our perception of reality and all that we *ever* see is simply reflected light off objects. My reflection in the mirror is not really me, but a reflection of light bounced off me. Einstein phrased the question of the mirror in quite a different manner. He pondered whether he would disappear if light struck him and his image in the mirror at precisely the same time.

AN OCCULT TRUTH

As mentioned earlier, the seventeenth-century mathematician Gottfried Wilhelm Leibniz saw all of creation divided neatly into two camps. One contained God above. The lower world was the world of illusion below him, and it operated as he ordained it. In the Leibniz universe, God exists in a realm of spirit with noncomposite, immaterial, soul-like entities called "monads." The illusions of our material world are, nonetheless, well founded and explained by the true nature of the universe at its fundamental level. For Leibniz, time does not really exist, but is the conceptual order that our minds put on existence. It only seems orderly for us to impose arbitrary terms like *sooner* or *later*.

This dichotomy of spirit and material realms also seemed most important to occult author Helena Petrovna Blavatsky. According to Blavatsky, the secret books that her Himalayan masters shared with her carried on the ancient mystery traditions and wisdom traditions that transcend religion, philosophies, and science. She called it the divine plan. Blavatsky's *The Secret Doctrine* and its description of the nature of humanity and the nature of the universe has both created controversy and inspired many people through the years. Her claim that she corresponded with the mysterious masters as her teachers was challenged and led to the formation of the Society for Psychical Research to debunk paranormal claims in England. However, her letters from the Mahatmas were examined, and it was determined by the Society for Psychical Research that they were not forgeries. These "Mahatma Letters" now reside in the British Museum. In *The Secret Doctrine* (vol. 1, page 83), Blavatsky writes of the dichotomy between the world of energy/spirit and the world of matter, drawing on ancient mystic texts:

> Father-Mother spin a web whose upper end is fastened to spirit—the light of the one darkness—and the lower one to matter (its shadowy end); and this web is the Universe spun out of the two substances made in one, which is Swabhavat.

Blavatsky introduced Westerners to the word *swabhavat* to describe self-becoming, the first cosmic monad, and the reflection of the primal, divine monad above us. She also said that swabhavat is the first manifestation of cosmic life when—at the end of the universal *pralaya* (great era)—the cry goes forth on the watchtower of eternity, "Let there be manifestation and light!"

All of creation, according to Blavatsky's occult teaching, is in a constant state of becoming, as energy becomes matter and matter becomes energy. From atom to snowflake, the same life force shapes all and inhabits all, propelling life and shaping it. Hence Blavatsky speaks of the Oneness of All. All of life is evolving, as we are evolving, in cycles of completion and renewal. This can be viewed as a returning to Spirit. This absolute reality, Blavatsky said, shapes all and unifies all, as all parts of the whole are interrelated and interdependent.

As we have seen, Blavatsky said that this universal life force runs through all of creation as a primal force called fohat. This was originally a Tibetan term, which represents the active or male potency of the female reproductive power (*sakti* in Sanskrit) that is found in nature. Blavatsky considered fohat to be the universal, propelling vital force behind everything. In human beings, fohat takes the form of subtle energy bodies as well as activating the physical body.

OUR ENERGY BODIES

The active belief in a human energy body that is separate from the physical body comes from the ancient Hindu tradition of yoga in India, but is certainly not limited to that culture. In fact, a great many religions around the world believe in some form of subtle energy body that can transcend our physical boundaries. According to esoteric, mystical teachings at the core of many wisdom traditions, the psycho-spiritual energy body corresponds to a subtle plane of existence. That subtle energy level of our existence is just one layer of the total makeup of human identity in a holistic view of the whole person. The belief in a human subtle energy body is found in Sufism, Chinese Taoism, Tibetan Buddhism, numerous shamanic folk religions, and even Christianity. We see in Christianity the "resurrection body" and the "glorified body." The mystic Sufis refer to the "most sacred body" and "supra-celestial body." In Taoism and Vajrayana, the subtle energy body is called "the diamond body." In Tibetan Buddhism, it is called the "rainbow body." The mystic Hermetic tradition refers to "the body of bliss" and "the immortal body." Martial arts' instruction includes special visualization exercises and breathing techniques to manipulate and direct the flow of energy forces within us to attain amazing powers beyond the common physical experience. And, of course, many shamanic traditions from America to New Zealand speak of "walking outside the physical body in a spirit body to visit the spirit realms above us."

In the Hindu Vedantic tradition, the subtle energy body includes five layers that sheath the physical body. The subtle body is the vehicle of consciousness that carries a person outside the physical body, as experienced by everyone in dying and passing into the next life. It includes a wide range of operation, from basic sensory perception to the eternal consciousness of a transmigrating entity.

Madame Blavatsky, influenced by her Eastern mystic masters, adopted much of Vedantic and yoga philosophy with regard to the subtle, multilayered body. She saw the subtle bodies or vehicles of consciousness outside our physical body as including the following:

- An etheric double or astral body (closest to our physical form)
- A desire form (extending outward from the astral body)
- A mental body, including higher mind (extending beyond the desire body)
- A consciousness or spiritual soul (extending beyond the mental body)

These subtle bodies became extended into six bodies (plus the physical, dense body) to correspond with seven planes of existence. From the inside (our dense, material body) outward, they are:

1. Material plane (our material body)
2. Etheric or astral plane (emotional body used in astral travel or astral projection)
3. Mental plane (our mental body, also employed in out-of-body projection)
4. Causal plane (our human insight, soul, causal body)
5. Buddha plane (our individualized consciousness)
6. Spiritual plane (energized conscious awareness entering universal consciousness)
7. The divine plane (our divine spirit; our connection to divinity)

Later Theosophical variations by C. W. Leadbeater and Annie Besant, among others, differentiated the etheric or astral body from an emotional body just outside it and combined the spiritual plane of universal consciousness or the oversoul with the divine plane. These are minute distinctions, of course. This arrangement, in which human subtle energy bodies are matched with planes of existence, was refined by the psychic author Alice Bailey, as well as Rudolph Steiner, Max Heindel, Barbara Brenner, and others, as the subtle bodies found their way into popular New Age philosophy. This new consciousness movement put an emphasis on chakras, energy centers that correspond to our seven bodies, and on auras as colorful manifestations of their energy output. These colorful manifestations of energy are reportedly visible to many clairvoyants.

The invisible astral body or etheric double was even known to the ancient Greeks in Hermetic tradition as a double to the human physical body. It more or less conforms to our material shape and size as a body double when operating out of body as a doppelganger or bioplasmic energy body. This astral body double can separate and project from the physical body. This body wraps tightly with the physical body, so that it envelops the material body. Valentina and Semyon Kirlian, with their Kirlian camera that measured auras or radiation discharge from the body, advanced this research into what they called bioplasma as human energy leaving the body.

We are much more than reflections of light bounced off our material bodies or reflections in a mirror. We are light beings. Electromagnetic radiation (light) dwells within us. This conclusion has been forming since the early 1800s and the early observations of Franz Anton Mesmer, who suggested that an electromagnetic field might exist around the human body and that the power of this electromagnetic field might be exerted to influence the energy field of another. He found that this human electromagnetic field showed many properties similar to the electromagnetic field described by James Maxwell in the early 1800s.

Then in the twentieth century Walter Kilner, a medical doctor at St. Thomas Hospital in London, reported seeing the human energy field, which he called an *aura*. He examined it with glass screens stained with dicyanin dye. He described the human energy field as three distinct zones around the physical body: one a quarter inch from the physical body, the next an inch from the body, and another six inches away. He published his study, *The Human Aura,* in 1965 in New York.

Later Dr. John C. Pierrakos and Eva Pierrakos, in a 1977 paper on bioenergetics, described the human energy field as light emissions from the human body. John Pierrakos went on to publish the groundbreaking book *Core Energetics.*

In similar research, Dr. Robert Becker of Upstate Medical School outlined a complex human electrical field that was shaped like the physical body and its central nervous system. He described his findings in 1962 in "The Direct Current Control System." Dr. Becker discovered that this field actually changes shape and intensity along with human psychological and physiological changes day-to-day. A decade later, further experiments by Dr. Becker discovered particles the size of electrons moving throughout this human electromagnetic field.

Later research by Dr. Safica Karagulla (*The Chakras and the Human Energy Fields*) and Dr. Larry Dossey (*Healing Words: The Power of Prayer and the Practice of Medicine*) brought even more clarity to the reality of the human energy field and the potentials of our light bodies.

Alchemical Taoism and the Fourth Way teachings of Gurdjieff and

Ouspensky suggest that we can even refine a subtle soul body through spiritual or yoga exercises to become a transcendent consciousness vehicle greater than what we naturally possess at birth. Aleister Crowley, author of *Magick without Tears,* suggests that our energy body or "body of light," as he called it, can be developed by discipline, rituals, and experience. We can pass through "the veil of the exterior world," he stated, as we create a "subtle body." This body, he said, "gains new powers as one progresses." Finally, he said, "One carries on almost one's whole life in this body of Light, and achieves in its own way the mastery of the Universe."

That mystic masters have done this is a matter of public record. Eck master Paul Twitchell's book *The Tiger's Fang* is his biographical account of his guru's out-of-body mystical journeys. Twitchell wrote the book in the 1950s for his master, Kirpal Singh, to collect the stories that his teacher brought back from his out-of-body journeys of discovery in deepest meditation. Between his first draft for publication in *Orion* magazine and later book forms Twitchell changed the name of the master in the book from Kirpal Singh to Sudar Singh and then later to Rebezar Tarzs. Regardless of the name changes, the accounts of a samadhi master who enters deepest meditation and leaves his body in a subtle, energy body of pure consciousness is a remarkable model and a classic biography. In this account, a man describes leaving his body and traveling beyond space and time, exploring various realms of existence beyond this physical world. He describes what it is like to enter the various planes of existence and what it is like to leave your physical body with your astral body, emotional body, mental body, and causal body. The inference is that various subtle bodies can travel with you outside your physical body.

LEAVING YOUR BODY TO EXPLORE THE PAST

If our human consciousness can leave our body and be directed as fast as the speed of light or even faster, as seen in thought-forms that instantly reach distant destinations, then we might logically assume that human consciousness can time travel. As light beings with electromagnetic energy that surrounds us and runs through us as dynamos of untapped power, we have the ability to travel at light speed or faster.

This possibility is supported by very serious studies in the practice of remote viewing, used even by the U.S. military and government in secret operations. As Einstein determined, time travel is possible when you exceed the speed of light. It is important to consider, however, that we cannot time travel as a physical body, but only as an energy body. When we separate our consciousness as pure energy to travel beyond our physical existence of the here and now, we go as witnesses with acute powers of conscious awareness. We have no physical form. We peek into exotic places—perhaps outside this physical world that we know. We can travel to another time with just a thought. Most people never imagine this to be truly possible, so do not make the journey in a state of higher consciousness. They do not see the possibilities that actually are boundless and endless.

Many out-of-body experiences in our expanding consciousness, of course, are not in exotic places like the places visited by Kirpal Singh, shamanic spirit walkers, or other mystics who explore the exotic planes of existence far beyond the here and now. Typically, we visit places that we know very well in our current sense of the time we occupy in our physical lives. Similarly, when we dream deeply and leave our body, we typically travel to places where we feel a personal attachment based on our experience. This is the only existence, the only reality that most of us believe we can access. But there is much more.

Where would you go? Most people would probably choose a time in the past—perhaps their own past-life situations, which now seem hopelessly gone and irretrievable. After all, most of us would have to admit that there's nothing more important to us than ourselves. That includes personal history, the pattern of our life, the baggage that we have picked up along the way, and how we got to where we are now.

Many people have argued that time travel into the past is impractical and therefore unlikely in an orderly universe, with the practical concern that you might murder your own grandparent or otherwise alter the course of events that brought you to the instant of your current physical reality. This possibility is entirely unlikely when you consider that the energy vehicle that brings you back in time is your consciousness and not your physical body. In a consciousness of pure energy, you have no physical form with which to interact physically in another time frame. You are invisible, without arms and legs. Even if you were able through training and experience to leave with various layers of your subtle energy body going forward with you, your out-of-body consciousness vehicle would still be invisible and without physical form. The etheric body, astral body, or doppelganger does assume a shape somewhat similar to our physical form, but is not perceived by most people (aside from the best clairvoyants, who have fine-tuned their conscious awareness beyond the five physical senses of common perception).

You go into the past as an observer or witness to the past and past events. This alone can be extremely insightful. In reviewing moments in your past, you can review scenes with a little detachment and a little distance from your initial involvement. Consequently, you would be able to see and understand with greater awareness to determine how events and moments in your past led to your current condition in your physical state. You can achieve the greatest goals of any human being: to know yourself, discover the patterns in life, and realize how past actions have affected you. You might also gain insight to your life purpose as you begin to see the patterns of the past with greater detachment and greater awareness. After all, history is what got you here, wherever "here" is.

You might still be wondering how you can get to where you need to go in the past. As we have discussed, you determine where and when to go in the past by visualization before you enter a state of meditation and higher consciousness. First you visualize where and when you want to go and paint a picture of what you want to do to carry with you into your meditation. This is focused intent. After you clear your mind and see only the blank slate in your mind's eye, the picture comes forward at the moment you enter into higher consciousness like a posthypnotic suggestion that you have given yourself. It becomes rather automatic. The picture you visualize doesn't even need to be precisely detailed, just as long as you understand it.

If you are time traveling to a specific instant in your own past life experience, then it becomes even easier. You have a karmic attraction to yourself, which is very much like electromagnetic attraction. Think how a magnet works so easily. The person in your past that you are visiting is exactly like you. Your conscious thought takes you back to that other you. You are instantly drawn together in a flash. If we consider that time is looped and not linear with a starting point, midpoint, and end line, then it's easy to see how the past you and the present you really exist simultaneously outside the space and fixed time of the mundane, physical world that holds us fast with its illusions of limitations.

You can also use higher states of consciousness to leave the body and explore other interesting moments in the past that are outside your own past life experience. You can examine the Crusades, an important coronation, or even the first flight of the Wright Brothers. Just visualize where and when you want to visit. You will not be able to interact, as you will have no physical body. You will, however, have profound awareness as an observer.

When you return to your physical body, you should have detailed recall of everything that you have seen. If you have trouble assembling what you have seen in the past, however, it might help to write down your memories from this experience as soon as possible. (This approach, incidentally, also works with dream recall, until you become good at controlled dreaming.) After you have written down your memories of the encounter, lie down and meditate on them, clearing your mind of everything else and tuning out outer distractions. Visualize the memories that you do recall in a picture format and then bring that picture with you into your meditation to examine.

LEAVING YOUR BODY
TO EXPLORE THE FUTURE

You can also explore the future in out-of-body time travel in a consciousness body. This is a little harder for most people to do because we have no frame of reference for the future. The future, after all, is an abstract concept for most of us. We have no memories or experience to guide us. Everything in the future seems so fuzzy. How can we visualize it and actually go there when it doesn't even exist yet? The answer, of course, is that the future already exists. The past, present, and future are all on the same time loop and exist simultaneously. It's simply our linear thinking and lack of perception that prevent us from escaping the illusion of fixed dimensions and frozen possibilities in the physical reality where we ordinarily live our simple lives.

Visionaries among us find their way into the future for glimpses of what awaits us. They become prophets for the rest of the world, alerting us to the future. Dreams of premonition are obvious results of time travel into the future. During my radio interviews about an earlier dream book, people often called in to relate their dreams of premonition with clear and accurate visions of the future. These were often very aware people who practiced controlled or lucid dreaming. In a sense, then, they were entering a meditative state and leaving their bodies in what is often called a "vivid dream." For many novices in the samadhi tradition of deep meditation states outside the body and outside space and time, controlled dreaming is a first level of meditation training. Maybe it's easier to think of these out-of-body journeys beyond space and time as dreams, like a movie we create in our imagination. There is no frame of reference for us to readily accept out-of-body travel.

When we leave our bodies and time travel into the future, writing down our memories of these experiences and then mediating on the images that we recall is even more necessary than when we time travel into the past. Again, this is because we have no frame of reference to deal with these visions of the future. They are *futuristic*, which for most of us sounds like science fiction. Thinking analytically with the tiny pocket calculator that is our control-freak brain, we often dismiss these visions of the future as not real because they have not happened yet in our frame of reference. Consequently, we think that they are only an imaginative concept of what might occur or might not.

But always remember that the past, present, and future occur simultaneously on one time line. Time is looped. Time is elastic. When we have visions of the future in a state of heightened consciousness and step outside the physical illusions of fixed time and space, we are seeing reality that is just as real and alive as what we call the present time or the past. We are expanding our awareness of reality beyond the flat-world, boxed-in dimensions that restrict our mundane view of the physical world at this instant.

MERGING TIME LINES

We tend to think of the future as one time line and the past as another distant time line. But there is only one time line, which is fluid. Nature is a good teacher of this principle, as Madame Blavatsky acknowledged in her classic little book *The Voice of the Silence*. Nature teaches us how the past becomes the future. We can see that trees do not die in autumn. Instead, they begin a regeneration process. In the winter, when much of the physical world is frozen, we commonly think of death. But the life force in nature endures and recycles. The next spring looks like the spring of last year. We, too, are essentially a life force—a light body encased in a gross, material body. We reside there, but we are not destined to remain entombed in our physical structures forever.

If we think of time occurring at the instant light energy strikes us, time appears to come in waves of primal energy that roll toward us, one right after the other. However, just as the waves of the ocean have a sequential pattern yet are all interrelated and part of the one great body of water, the rays of the sun that strike each one of us in succession, energizing and giving each of us our sense of the moment, are really *one ray* that has been refracted and dispersed as many beautiful rays of light.

It is one uninterrupted flow of energy, bringing time waves in unceasing succession to all of life in its flow.

While people might have a sense of "sooner" and "later," as Leibniz said, all time lines flow as one. We can ride the time line like a wave that takes us anywhere we want to go, merging with moments in the distant past or moments in the future, as we commonly think of it. We have already lived in this future, as the future occurs simultaneously with the past and present. It is not alien to us. We are welcome there as light moving forward.

It might help to think of a subway system, such as the London Circle Line. You can get in this underground tube and go one direction or the other direction. Ultimately, the line makes a complete circuit through the city, however, and takes you everywhere along the line and eventually back to where you started. Similarly, you can start now and go anywhere along the great, eternal time line, backward or forward, just like hopping aboard a subway. You decide where you want to go. Think of the physical barriers that restrict your escape from this frozen, material world of fixed time without change and significant movement as being like a subway gate that keeps would-be travelers without tickets from passing to the waiting trains. It's not that hard to gain entrance, however. Just put yourself in the state of consciousness of a would-be traveler and escape this material world of the here and now, with its limited possibilities.

Some exercises will help you.

VISITING YOUR OWN PAST

What You Need

- A quiet, enclosed room in which to meditate without distractions.
- A mat, pad, or blanket on which to recline on your back to meditate.
- Loose-fitting clothing, with your shoes removed.

Procedure

1. Recline on your back with arms and legs outstretched (yoga's dead man posture).

2. Tune out all external distractions and internal thoughts, finding the quiet still point deep within you. Begin deep, controlled breathing.

3. Visualize a place and time in your own past that you intend to visit. Perhaps you will select a time that was pivotal to your development or a time of confusion that has bothered you. You decide. Let the picture of this scene form in your mind's eye with details.

4. When you sense a real connection with this scene, tuck this picture away in the back of your consciousness to retrieve when you reach a state of heightened consciousness in a meditative state.

5. Now visualize leaving your body to visit this time and place as soon as you reach a state of higher consciousness in your deep meditation. Tuck that picture away in the back of your consciousness to retrieve as soon as you are ready.

6. Tune out all internal thought and distractions and put your physical body to sleep as your lower mind gives way to your higher consciousness.

7. When you see the blank slate in your mind's eye, focus on it, then bring forward your intent to leave your body to visit a time and place in your past. Then bring forward your visualization of the precise time and place you intend to visit.

8. If your visualization was properly formed and your intent properly focused, you should find yourself instantly transported to the precise time and place you selected.

9. When you arrive there, look all around you to observe details, including your own presence.

10. Become a perfect witness to history by observing everything with detachment. You will not be seen or noticed, as you have no physical body. Your keen new awareness in this pure consciousness body, however, will enable you to see, hear, and otherwise perceive what you observe. Do not attempt to analyze.

11. When you have seen what you came to observe, return to your physical body by thinking of that body and returning to it.

12. When back in your physical body, slowly adjust to your return from this deep out-of-body meditation.

13. Write down your observations, remembering your experience out of time and space. Remember the scene as a detailed picture.

14. Return to the reclining posture and meditate on what you have observed in your out-of-body travel into the past. This is the time for analysis, with physical detachment. It is the perfect way to interpret what you have encountered.

EXPLORING A PAST LIFE

What You Need

• A quiet, enclosed room in which to meditate without distractions.

• A mat, pad, or blanket on which to recline on your back to meditate.

• Loose-fitting clothing, with your shoes removed.

Procedure

1. Recline on your back with arms and legs outstretched.

2. Tune out all external distractions and internal thoughts, finding the quiet still point deep within you. Begin deep, controlled breathing.

3. Visualize a place and time you lived before this lifetime. It might help you to think back to when you were a baby and then focus on a time before then. It might not be possible to actually picture a detailed time and place you lived previously. Just visualize a time before this lifetime. Tuck that basic image in the back of your consciousness to call forward when you enter heightened consciousness and are ready to leave your physical body.

4. Visualize leaving your physical body when you have reached higher consciousness and then tuck that formed intent as a picture in the back of your consciousness.

5. Tune out all internal thoughts and distractions and put your physical body to sleep as your lower mind gives way to your higher consciousness.

6. When you see the blank slate in your mind's eye, focus on it, then bring forward your intent to leave your body to visit a time and place in your distant past. Then bring forward your visualization of the precise time and place you intend to visit.

7. If your visualization was properly formed and your intent properly focused,

you should find yourself instantly transported to the precise time and place you selected.

8. When you arrive there, look all around you to observe details, including your own presence. You might not recognize yourself in this previous physical incarnation at first.

9. Become a perfect witness to history by observing everything with detachment. You will not be seen or noticed, as you have no physical body. Your keen new awareness in this pure consciousness body, however, will enable you to see, hear, and otherwise perceive what you observe. Do not attempt to analyze.

10. When you have seen what you came to observe, return to your physical body by thinking of that body and returning to it.

11. Back in your physical body, slowly adjust to your return from this deep out-of-body meditation.

12. Write down your observations, remembering your experience out of time and space. Remember the scene as a detailed picture.

13. Return to the reclining posture and meditate on what you have observed in your out-of-body travel into the past. This is the time for analysis, with physical detachment. It is the perfect way to interpret what you have encountered.

EXPLORING HISTORY

What You Need

- A quiet, enclosed room in which to meditate without distractions.
- A mat, pad, or blanket on which to recline on your back to meditate.
- Loose-fitting clothing, with your shoes removed.

Procedure

1. Recline on your back with arms and legs outstretched.

2. Tune out all external distractions and internal thoughts, finding the quiet still point deep within you. Begin deep, controlled breathing.

3. Visualize a place and time in the history of the world that you would like to experience. This could be any time and any place in history that

fascinates you and calls to you to experience it for yourself. It does not matter that it is something outside your own life experience. Form a picture of this scene as best you can and then tuck it in the back of your consciousness with the intent to bring it forward when you reach higher consciousness and are ready to leave your physical body.

4. Visualize leaving your physical body when you have reached higher consciousness and tuck that intent in the back of your consciousness as a picture to bring forward as soon as you are ready.

5. Tune out all internal thought and distractions and put your physical body to sleep as your lower mind gives way to your higher consciousness.

6. When you see the blank slate in your mind's eye, focus on it, then bring forward your intent to leave your body to visit a time and place in the past. Then bring forward your visualization of the precise time and place you intend to visit.

7. If your visualization was properly formed and your intent properly focused, you should find yourself instantly transported to the precise time and place you selected.

8. When you arrive there, look all around you to observe details. Your own presence in this instance will likely be restricted to your pure consciousness body, unless you surprise yourself by finding yourself to have been an active participant in this moment in history. (We are often drawn to moments in history that might have more personal connection to ourselves than we realize. Perhaps you are seeing yourself in a previous incarnation.)

9. Become a perfect witness to history by observing everything with detachment. You will not be seen or noticed, as you have no physical body. Your keen new awareness in this pure consciousness body, however, will enable you to see, hear, and otherwise observe everything there. Do not attempt to analyze.

10. When you have seen what you came to observe, return to your physical body by thinking of that body and returning to it.

11. Back in your physical body, slowly adjust to your return from this deep out-of-body meditation.

12. Write down your observations, remembering your experience out of time and space. Remember the scene as a detailed picture.

13. Return to the reclining posture and meditate on what you have observed in your out-of-body travel into the past. This is the time for analysis, with physical detachment. It is the perfect way to interpret what you have encountered.

VISITING YOUR OWN FUTURE

What You Need

• A quiet, enclosed room in which to meditate without distractions.

• A mat, pad, or blanket on which to recline on your back to meditate.

• Loose-fitting clothing, with your shoes removed.

Procedure

1. Recline on your back with arms and legs outstretched.

2. Tune out all external distractions and internal thoughts, finding the quiet still point deep within you. Begin deep, controlled breathing.

3. Visualize a place and time in the future that will involve you. This will not be easy, perhaps. You have no ready form of reference that you can recognize. The blank slate in your mind's eye might remain blank at first. Stay with your focused intent to visualize your future. You are not looking here into the distant future with all of its many possibilities, but only your own immediate future. What comes next for you? Slowly the picture will begin to come into focus in your mind's eye. When the picture is formed, even vaguely (and it will most likely be vague), simply tuck that picture in the back of your consciousness with the intent to retrieve it when you reach higher consciousness and begin to leave your physical body.

4. Now visualize leaving your physical body when you have reached higher consciousness and tuck that intent in the back of your consciousness as a picture to bring forward as soon as you are ready.

5. Tune out all internal thought and distractions and put your physical body to sleep as your lower mind gives way to your higher consciousness.

6. When you see the blank slate in your mind's eye, focus on it, then bring

forward your intent to leave your body to visit a time and place in your future. Then bring forward your visualization of the precise time and place you intend to visit.

7. If your visualization was properly formed and your intent properly focused, you should find yourself instantly transported to the precise time and place you selected.

8. When you arrive there, look all around you to observe details, including your own presence. You will be able to sense your own presence in your pure consciousness body, but may have difficulty finding your future self. Stay with it, however, until you sense the presence of your future self. Your spirit should be drawn to itself like a magnet, even in the future.

9. Become a perfect witness to what you see there by observing everything with detachment. You will not be seen or noticed, as you have no physical body. Your keen new awareness in this pure consciousness body, however, will enable you to see, hear, and otherwise perceive what you observe. Do not attempt to analyze.

10. When you have seen what you came to observe, return to your physical body by thinking of that body and returning to it.

11. Back in your physical body, slowly adjust to your return from this deep out-of-body meditation.

12. Write down your observations, remembering your experience out of time and space. Remember the scene as a detailed picture.

13. Return to the "dead man" reclining posture and meditate on what you have observed in your out-of-body travel into the future. This is the time for analysis, with physical detachment. It is the perfect way to interpret what you have encountered

LOOKING INTO THE WORLD TOMORROW

Using the same visualization and meditation approach as in the "Visiting Your Own Future" exercise above, travel outside your physical body to the future to examine how things are different in the world. This time your visit will not be specifically personal, with an eye on yourself, but a time traveler's observation of what the future holds in general for our physical world. You might want to prepare yourself before you depart with various visualizations on different aspects of the world that might change in the future.

You might be surprised by what you find. Some things about this physical world might change much less than you would imagine. Remember always that this physical world is the realm of material form and therefore less able to undergo significant change than the unmanifest realm of energy. Nonetheless, you will find many things different in the future that you visit.

Sixth Secret of Time

HEALING OUTSIDE OF TIME AND BECOMING AN ENERGIZED CHANGE AGENT

Stepping outside space and time allows the out-of-body time traveler to heal and effect real change in ways that would seem impossible in the mundane, material world. Once outside the restrictions of our fixed, physical world and the realm of manifest creation, we can move more freely in the unmanifest realm of energy with unlimited possibilities. We can move faster with greater awareness. We are not limited by our five poor senses and the three dimensions of our gross, mundane world. Moving beyond the realm where energy has been frozen into rigid, solid form, our pure consciousness moves with lightning speed and makes changes with the slightest desire of our thoughts to bend pliable energy to our will.

Traveling outside time and space in a pure consciousness body as energy has many practical applications. We can use this out-of-body experience (OBE) to visit various individuals in various situations in what might be called *remote viewing*. The subtle bodies that we take with us in OBE travel assist us in our role as skillful witnesses of what we observe. The greatest use of this sort of OBE remote viewing for us personally, however, could be observing illness in our physical bodies and those of loved ones. We can diagnose problems, do distant healing or astral healing, better deal with recovery and addictions, reach higher understanding, project our healing thoughts, soul travel, accomplish soul retrieval, bi-locate, and listen to universal intelligence. The key to all of this, as we have seen, resides in deep meditation, where we reach higher consciousness and leave our restricted physical body.

HEALING OUTSIDE OUR BODIES

Going outside our physical bodies gives us special opportunities for observation with a bird's eye view and detachment. Even more significant is the lack of physical limitations outside the physical realm. When we go into a deep meditation with the focused intent of leaving our physical bodies as pure consciousness, we move in our energy bodies at the speed of light or faster. Consequently, we slow down the perception of time. The fixed laws of physics in our physical world of matter do not exist outside space and time where our energy bodies go. The unmanifest side of creation where our energy bodies take us is a different world of fluid possibilities and infinite potential for change, where desire transforms energy into new matter.

Stepping outside our bodies to heal in the respected tradition of the shamanic dream walker enables us to reach beyond the limitations of the fixed, restricted world into a new world of abundant potential for change. This can happen in the twinkling of an eye, as consciousness as energy rethinks and reforms free of any restrictions of the gross, mundane world of rigidity. Working outside physical restrictions also allows us to see the many layers of our suffering beyond obvious broken bones, cuts, and sores. As out-of-body energy healers, we are able to look more clearly into the emotional, physical, mental, and spiritual ailments of our subtle bodies that physical healers generally cannot perceive and often do not consider.

At one time or another every one of us has experienced the limitation of physicians in seeing only our surface problems. This is hardly their fault, as they are doing the very best they can to deal with physical symptoms and physical problems. They are dealing with layers of problems that manifest themselves ultimately throughout the entire human system, including the physical layer of our total being—the only layer of our being that they perceive. They do not readily see the subtle emotional, mental, causal, and spiritual bodies that complete us and make us whole.

Fortunately for all of us, allopathic medicine has recently evolved from its origins of meatball surgery and pill-pushing to more of a holistic practice. As a result, more medical doctors now also consider emotional, mental, and spiritual ailments, although they tend to treat them independently. Nonetheless, modern Western medicine is beginning to recognize the effects of emotional and spiritual illness on the physical body, even though these subtle ailments are considered separately by different caregivers and not seen as part of an interrelated, interdependent body of energy grids.

The energy healer who seeks to help can effect real change by helping the sick to heal on their own, recognizing that each person is an electromagnetic dynamo that has temporarily lost its ability to regenerate. This does not put the energy healer in the capacity of a physician, because the healer does not operate in the same way as a medical doctor. Rather, the energy healer sends healing thoughts to assist a sick friend to heal on his own or her own. Our healing thoughts, after all, are pure energy. These thoughts are delivered by our pure energy body of consciousness, sent at the speed of light outside space and time. Here there are no limitations. Here miraculous healing and significant change is possible.

DIAGNOSING PROBLEMS

When we say that an energy healer can leave the physical body in deep meditation to diagnose health problems, we do not mean *diagnose* in the same way that medical doctors use the term. Energy healers do not make specific medical diagnoses, which they might not be medically trained and licensed to do. Rather, they observe what they are able to perceive with their out-of-body conscious awareness and report back to their sick friend what conditions might require follow-up medical attention. What makes this possible and very special is that when we leave the body as pure energy our limited perceptive skills as three-dimensional thinkers with five poor physical senses are replaced with conscious awareness that is much keener.

When we visit a sick friend (always with his or her permission first), our higher consciousness connects instantly with that of our friend. This connection, it must be emphasized, is spirit to spirit. When we make this kind of connection, soul to soul, we can sense instantly where problems reside and the extent of the problems as they spread through the whole human being.

As energy healers we have a greater awareness and recognition of anomalies in the layers of our human existence. It is essentially the same with our pets and other animals—even our houseplants, trees, and crops in the field. All organic life-forms are multilayered, with subtle energy bodies that are interrelated and interconnected. In a pure consciousness body, we can travel anywhere and see that. All life-forms are essentially alike, as energy beings wrapped in layers around physical casements that hold us down.

The real beauty of being able to escape the normal time and space of this physical world is probably not in the exotic and revealing things that you can see and experience, but in all of the good you can do for others and even yourself in terms of effecting real healing. You don't always need to go that far, either. You can go outside your physical body and observe yourself. In such case, you will simply hover over your physical body, which is resting in a meditative state, and make your conscious observations there in the same space and time.

We can hurt on many levels in ways that impact us on all levels of our being, as emotional, mental, and spiritual problems descend to our densest level of physical pain and unknown suffering. As we travel out of body as pure conscious energy, our newfound powers of awareness will exceed any powers of perception that anyone in a physical body can readily bring to bear on our deepest health problems.

Even energy healers in their physical bodies have less powers of conscious awareness. Anyone who travels outside his or her body with focused intent achieves a higher level of conscious awareness as pure energy, no longer bound by the restrictions of the physical world. Consequently, anyone can become a very skillful healer and observe what really ails us through deep, focused meditation that takes him or her outside the physical body.

Once you have left your physical body and made your observations with regard to a sick friend, pet, or even yourself, you should quickly write down exactly what you recall and then meditate on it. Do not excessively analyze things. That is always the approach that our analytical brain favors. What we have observed in higher consciousness outside the body cannot always relate to normal frames of reference that are comfortable for our rational lower mind to process and resolve. Do not verbalize internally, either, as you meditate on what you have observed. Rather, picture what you have observed in your mind's eye as a complete scene with your impressions. What did you sense?

After you have jotted down your observations and meditated on them, relay this information to your friend as advice for possible follow-up with professional, licensed caregivers. Do not put any particular value or slant on the information, but simply relay what you believe you have observed. Once again, all of this is done only with the permission of your friend. It is unethical to spy on people without their permission or intercede without their consent. Also, it is unethical to give advice unless it is desired.

In the case of a sick pet or sick plant that you might have observed, refer the pet or plant in question to its owner for possible professional follow-up on your concerns. If the pet is yours, then you should present your concerns to the pet's veterinarian. In the case of your own plant, you might present your concerns to a horticulturist, botanist, or plant consultant.

It is not always necessary or advisable to tell professional caregivers how you made your observations. They might not understand and might find all of this a bit incredible. Simply tell them that you have a feeling about how things are or might be. Then ask them to look into it for you. Never be reluctant to ask for outside assistance, especially when your concerns are for others in pain.

DISTANT HEALING

It is possible to send your healing thoughts to someone at great distance and reach him or her instantaneously because your thoughts are directed, pure energy that is laced with the focused intent to help and heal. Your thoughts leave your body and the physical limitations of the manifest world as energy released into the unmanifest world. Your thoughts will find their mark with amazing accuracy due to karmic attraction that operates like two ends of electromagnets that are instantly drawn together without reservation. Sending our healing thoughts, if directed with this sort of focused intent, is a wondrous thing that any of us can do.

In keeping with our discussion of out-of-body travel outside normal space and time, however, we would like to outline what is involved in *astral healing*, whereby a person travels in an astral or subtle energy body and reaches a sick friend or pet with a presence that includes conscious awareness as an observer.

In ancient Eastern mystic schools and the honorable practice of yoga, the concept and practice of leaving the body in a state of deep, higher consciousness is commonplace. There are many ways to think of the traveling vehicle that carries our consciousness outside the physical body. You might think of the traveling body as your *etheric double*. The etheric plane on the outer body is often seen as an invisible, subtle energy layer that interconnects the astral body to the physical body like an envelope that acts as our health aura as it connects the energy of our many outer subtle bodies to our dense, physical body. It is often commonly called our *double*.

Another way of looking at this traveling body is that our astral subtle body and mental subtle body leave the physical body in a combination of emotional and mental energy or the emotional subtle body and mental subtle body. Yet another way of looking at this traveling body comes from yoga and the creation of an *illusory body* as an expression of the subtle bodies. This illusory energy body is created by the practice of visualizing it in a mirror until one becomes comfortable with the idea of a second body. Still another way of looking at our out-of-body traveling vehicle comes from traditional Hinduism's Vedantic philosophy. The Vedantic view is that our one subtle body has many *kosas*, or sheaths. The *linga sarira* traveling body is seen in Samkhya, Vedanta, and yoga studies as the vehicle of consciousness.

My own view—based on practical experience in samadhi mysticism, Eckankar soul travel, and shamanic dream walking—is that we can leave our physical bodies with pure energy consciousness with various levels of our being. We can leave with an astral body or can also take the mental body, causal body, or higher spiritual bodies of individualized consciousness and universal consciousness along for the ride. Taking all levels of your higher self with you adds to your experience with more energy and more insight. This is a way of saying that there are many aspects to our total being as energy life-forms, and embracing all of our total being improves our effectiveness.

However you conceive of that part of your subtle energy that travels with your consciousness out of body, you should remember that only gifted clairvoyants will ever see your invisible spirit body. What they see, from most accounts, will be a physical outline that greatly resembles your physical body, with the impression of slightly greater size. Some people might see you as something like light, and that's a pretty fair description of your energy body as electromagnetic radiation that travels at the speed of light. Your loved ones who have a very close connection to you might sense your presence to some degree, even if they are unable to see you at all.

As astral healers we visit the sick—with their permission—to observe their illness and reach out to them with healing energy. In our consciousness body, we come to them as pure energy. We can also tap into the energy that is all around us as electromagnetic radiation. With no analytical thought, our conscious awareness senses the anomaly in our sick friends and reaches out to them with an energy boost to help restore their health. This might sound intrusive, but it's no more intrusive than a handshake or a hug. As we connect spirit to spirit, we have an instinctive awareness of what is needed in terms of energy to help our friends on their way to self-recovery. We do not set bones, alter their internal chemistry, or anything else that would be considered physical tampering. Giving them energy is a loving and simple way to assist them. Giving them energy with the focused intent to help them heal cannot hurt or stifle them in any way. This is universal energy, something that they were born with. We introduce nothing alien to them.

The process is simple and quick. A little energy goes a long way toward boosting their chances of recovery. Think of this like visiting the sick with a little good cheer. You are just bringing them your energy. Once you have reached out to them with a little energy projected with your focused intent to heal, then you can turn your attention back to your physical presence and return to your body, which is reclining in deep meditation.

RECOVERY

We can also assist people—ourselves included—who have trouble with recovery from longtime addictions, predispositions, and patterned tendencies as lingering afflictions that cripple us on many levels. These are difficult cases, because the ailment is not simply apparent on the physical level. Often there are deep-rooted problems on emotional, mental, causal, and spiritual levels that go very deep into a person's past as a soul with many lives and many layers of being. Speaking to the analytical lower mind is like talking to the confused captain of a ship of fools. Looking for physical or psychological keys to recovery can seem shortsighted. The truth of the matter is that many people with deep-seated addictions, predispositions, or troubled tendencies in their lives find it hard to recover.

We carry a lot of baggage, and it isn't all physical and psychological. Around our corporeal body we carry many layers of transcendent, subtle bodies with invisible baggage. Perhaps it would be easier to deal with the baggage that hinders our recovery if we could see it. If we had a determined leech attached to our back that was noticeably affecting our posture and gait, it might be easier to determine how to remove our lingering problem. But the sort of leeches that we carry around in our emotional, mental, causal, and spiritual subtle bodies are not that obvious, even though they drain our overall energy field. They represent very old, invisible wounds that are unknown to the rational mind, even on a subconscious level. They are not necessarily traceable to any obvious moment in our physical past, but often come from a distant past in a former life or from a subtle body level of which our lower mind memory is not even aware.

Our spirit bodies as pure energy live forever and have history that predates our physical bodies. It's realistic to think that the eternal spirit part of us that endures beyond physical life carries old wounds. Attempting to heal longtime wounds on subtle body levels by treating the physical core or dealing psychologically with the lower mind is a bit like a blind person trying to identify an elephant by feeling an isolated wrinkle or two. What kind of therapy can treat invisible leeches that drain our energy on such subtle body levels? Does your psychologist offer it? Does your medical doctor? Does your therapist? The only way to determine what is wrong is to visit where the problem resides to observe it. We can only visit problems that reside in our subtle energy bodies by going outside our physical bodies to observe. Once we are aware of the problem and where it resides, then we can treat it.

All of us have known or seen people who valiantly try to cope with addictive tendencies, predispositions, and dangerous patterns in their lives with little success of recovery. Many drug addicts never turn their lives around. Only some 25 percent of cocaine addicts who undergo treatment programs in the United States ever really recover; many continue to go through treatment programs again and again. It is the same with alcoholics and many other people with addictive patterns. It is much the same, also, for people who continue to have what we might consider bad luck or accidents as an unfortunate pattern in their lives. Sometimes we call this bad karma. This is the result of invisible baggage that we carry around us on many subtle levels of our being. Recovery is possible, but only with understanding that a better perspective offers. Going outside our physical bodies in higher consciousness gives us the sort of higher awareness we need to see what is not obvious. Once we have connected with these invisible leeches that prevent our recovery, we can reach out with healing energy to assist our loved ones with their recovery.

SHAMANIC SOUL RETRIEVAL

In the shamanic tradition of spirit walking, a person enters a deep trance-like state of meditation and leaves the body to explore the past for clues to the future. The spirit walker might seek healing for a person by retrieving things that have been lost in his or her past. We can consider these lost bits of things in our past as little pieces of ourselves, which have been taken from us and left behind, leaving us incomplete and not whole. This healing activity is commonly called *shamanic soul retrieval*. In this ancient practice, the healer goes back into key moments in your past when you lost, gave away, or were robbed of pieces of your soul.

Venturing outside the body to search for parts of our soul or essential life force that have been lost in our life journey is something that any of us could do, if willing and able to enter a state of higher consciousness. Theoretically, it would be easier for you to find lost parts of yourself than going through an intermediary. Relaying your ideas of where you have lost parts of your soul to another has the same loss of fidelity in communication that we see when we make a copy of something or a copy of a copy. There is nothing like communication from the source. You are the source. Nobody can find lost parts of you better than you can, if you know how to leave your body with focused intent and travel outside normal space and time. You have a natural karmic attraction to lost pieces of yourself and should be immediately drawn to your missing pieces.

Anyone who has read *The Secret Life of Plants, The Secret Life of Your Cells,* or *Secrets of the Soil* readily recognizes how missing parts of the whole can sense their fragmented parts regardless of distance and seclusion. This is exactly the way it works with us, too, when we give a part of our heart to someone or someone emotionally or mentally rips our guts out. People who have been close to us in our past have a spiritual connection to us and have a hold on us. The missing parts of our subtle energy bodies might not be obvious to the physical eye, but are readily felt as gaping holes in us that keep us from standing up straight and walking with confidence and real spirit. We have all lost pieces of ourselves everywhere along life's long journey. It can be the result of a relationship breakup. Perhaps we gave ourselves to someone or something to the extent that we have little left to give. As author Louis Gittner, an early teacher of mine, once told me, "Be careful when you give yourself to someone. People from our past often have a hold on us and can pull us this way and that, as though they have us on a string." This is not a physical hold, of course, but a hold on some part of our subtle energy bodies.

You also can lose a part of your life essence entirely on your own by leaving a part of yourself on a battlefield, a car accident, a traumatic encounter, or another dreadful time in your past when you limped away not completely whole. It's one thing if you lose a leg, but the scars of losing emotional energy, mental energy, or spiritual energy are much less obvious and just as debilitating. Speaking personally, I recall vividly being lost overnight in a dense forest and feeling that a part of me was still lost in that forest. Anyone who has been to war probably understands what it means to lose part of your spirit in the process. We are surrounded by the walking wounded, who look physically fine and yet feel disconnected and fragmented.

Reclaiming soul fragments requires thorough visualization of your desire to reclaim what you have lost, even if you don't readily know where to look. You can picture in your mind's eye what you believe you have lost, as best you can conceptualize. Then you can give yourself the suggestion to leave your physical body when you reach higher consciousness to retrieve this lost part of yourself. You will be magnetically drawn to it, like the positive and negative ends of two magnets that pull instantly toward each other. Once you find that lost part of yourself, you will instantly find yourself back in your physical body. The process can be repeated again and again as you visualize various parts of yourself that you sense you have lost. This might involve visiting people from your past or places where you have become fragmented. This is your own journey of self-discovery, and nobody really knows you better than yourself.

In this shamanic healing practice you revisit the moments when you lost a part of yourself, examine where you lost it, and reclaim it through your greater awareness in this state of higher consciousness. Thought power is a wonderful thing, especially in a state of higher consciousness.

BI-LOCATION

Occultist lore warns against coming face-to-face with your double when your life force or spirit travels outside your physical body. This would only be possible if you allowed your physical body to function during out-of-body travel, of course. We take all precautions to provide a safe resting place for our physical body when we enter deep meditation trances to leave our body in a higher consciousness vehicle. The physical body that is left behind should be tucked away in a secluded room or space where it will not be disturbed and can rest perfectly protected from the elements and outside influences.

Providing any smaller measure of safety for our physical body during meditation could worry your little brain to the extent it could feel insecure about releasing control during the short while that you tuck your body away in meditation. Its greatest concern, of course, is self-preservation. Consequently, we must assure our physical side that it will be safe and comfortable during our out-of-body meditation.

When your conscious vehicle goes outside your physical body to observe your own physical condition, this encounter of meeting your body's double does not constitute a face-to-face confrontation. Even if you looked into the face of your physical double, it would not constitute a meaningful encounter. That is because your physical body in its peaceful repose during meditation has no consciousness, but is totally asleep.

On the other hand, leaving your body while you continue to function as a physical being could be dangerous. If you become so comfortable popping out of your body in an instant and do not take proper precautions to establish a meditation place, then you could come face-to-face with your double. When I first became comfortable with leaving my body in a state of higher consciousness, I was thrilled with the adventure and practiced no self-control. The longing of the spirit to leave the body to explore on its own is the same for you and for everyone else. I only hope that you will practice self-control and not pop out of your body while you are walking down a busy street, walking in the woods at night, or working with chemicals in a dark enclosure, as I have done.

Bi-location might sound like fun, but it can be dangerous. There is a practical reason to worry about coming face-to-face with your double during an out-of-body experience. One of "you" has very focused awareness as an observer. That's the OBE double, of course. The other "you" is a physical being who has lost focus and is wandering out of control. Hopefully, your physical being has enough sensory perception and mental alertness to dodge cars and other dangers. On the other hand, it has tuned out a lot of sensory awareness and brain functions in order to release your consciousness. As a result, the physical self at that time is a sort of walking automaton functioning on a rudimentary level.

LISTENING TO
UNIVERSAL INTELLIGENCE

One of the greatest benefits from reaching a state of higher consciousness and *tuning out* all internal thought from our analytical brain is that we can *tune into* outside information on a universal scope. It is unlikely that we could do this without meditating and becoming alert observers. In deep meditation, we become excellent listeners with new powers of conscious awareness. In our normal condition as busy, engaged physical beings, we find ourselves swamped by nearby chatter that is distracting. Our five senses pick up everything within our immediate physical surroundings. We also find ourselves distracted by our own inner thoughts, which ramble aimlessly over concerns about past events and anxiety over future possibilities. In a sense, we spend most of our lives possessed by these phantoms.

In a deep meditative state, we clear our minds and tune out physical sensations to become perfect observers with invisible antennas raised far beyond the finite space that our physical bodies occupy. We become perfect receptors to universal intelligence once we learn to listen perfectly in this manner. All of the great thoughts that exist in the past, present, and future exist eternally as pure energy that continues to flow freely. Theoretically, radio waves from the past continue to travel freely around and around. All of the greatest music that has ever been performed or even conceived continues to flow freely. Much has been written about the special dimension that the world's greatest composers tap for inspiration. So perhaps our most inspired composers, inventors, writers, mathematicians, and engineers are better at taking dictation than creating anything new on their own.

When we desire significant change in our lives or real healing, we might find the best answers outside our physical world. Learning to leave your physical body in deep meditation allows you to visit a world of possibilities and universal intelligence beyond the finite world of noise and confusion that characterizes our material existence. We do not require our rational, analytical mind when we travel out of body. Your lower mind would not be much good to you, anyway, as it would have no frame of reference in this realm. What replaces your physical brain and normal physical sensory perception when you travel outside time and space is awareness of the higher consciousness as pure energy that allows you to tap into universal understanding of how things work. This makes us excellent observers with the power to effect significant change and healing from the unmanifest side of creation, where anything is possible and change is completely fluid.

SOME ETHICAL CONSIDERATIONS

There are ethical considerations to guide our out-of-body efforts. We must always remember to seek prior permission when we seek to observe people or conditions or seek to effect healing or other changes that will involve others. No, you will not need written permission. Realize, however, that full disclosure is ethically required so that your loved ones will know in advance that you plan to drop in on them and give their consent for you to do that. Their cooperation does not mean that they will play any active part or need to know exactly what you intend to do. Their participation is not required in any way. All that is required of them is their approval to let you visit them to try to help them.

Obviously, not everyone you know will comprehend what you

intend to do by leaving your physical body, nor will many people believe that you can accomplish this feat. It is not necessary for them to believe in what you claim you can do for them. On the other hand, almost everyone seems comfortable with the concept of sending healing thoughts and best wishes during times of illness or difficulty. So perhaps you can simply tell your friend that you would like to send healing energy to them and visit them in your dreams to help them, if you can. That might suffice as an explanation, and it happens to be a fairly accurate description of your intent.

With many loved ones, such as your pets, children, or spouse, you might have a sense of implied consent, based on your understanding of those who are near and dear to you. You probably have a closeness to these loved ones that makes even asking for permission unnecessary.

You might wonder why permission is even necessary when you intend only to help heal or bring about positive change for good. Aside from the issue of privacy, your out-of-body visit could be an intrusion that interferes with others' free will to determine what is best for themselves on their own. Many Eastern mystics have long worried about the karma that you could conceivably disrupt by altering the course of events in progress. Certainly every person and all living things in this physical world of ours are destined to die. It is sometimes difficult to determine when our time to die has come. Sometimes the course of events is irreversible. Sometimes we have lived a full life and reached our physical end. This is not a decision we can readily make for others. They get to decide. Ultimately, the sick heal themselves. The question is whether they want our assistance.

Even with the terminally ill, however, we can bring healing energy to reduce their pain and bring them greater peace and tranquility. We can bring healing energy to assist loved ones who have been struck down prematurely in accidents. How our loved ones process the energy that is available to them in their distress amounts to a personal decision, in any regard.

REMOTE HEALING

In this meditation, you should select a sick person or animal to visit. Distance and known location do not matter. Your loving thoughts will bring you directly to that person wherever he or she is. This is basic karmic attraction. However, if you wish to visit a friend, you should have his or her permission before extending healing assistance. Perhaps you would like to practice first on a pet.

What You Need
- A quiet, isolated room where you can shut yourself inside safely for a deep out-of-body meditation. (Always position your physical body in a clean, warm, safe place so that it will feel comfortable about releasing you as it peacefully rests.)
- Loose-fitting clothing, ideally with shoes removed.
- A mat, blanket, or pad on the ground on which to recline on your back (or a straight-backed chair if you prefer to meditate in a seated position with feet firmly on the ground, hands and feet uncrossed, and erect posture).

Procedure
1. Close the door and recline on the mat on your back with legs and arms extended to each side and eyes open. Begin deep, controlled breathing.
2. Visualize how you intend to leave your body and visit a pet or a sick friend who has given you permission to assist him or her by visiting in this way.
3. Now close your eyes and enter a meditative state, tuning out all external and internal distractions while letting your physical body become numb and restful.
4. When you enter a state of heightened consciousness in this deep, focused meditation, you will instantly leave your body, based on your visualized intent. The first time you do this remote healing meditation, you might sense that you are floating through space or you might find yourself instantly transported to your destination. The sense of moving through open space is a throwback to our physical frame of reference. In truth, you are traveling through space and time outside physical limitations.

5. When you find yourself with your loved one, look carefully around the room and note the details to assure yourself that you are truly present with your subject. It might surprise you at first how precisely you are able to discern what this loved one is doing, details of the location, and the actual situation you encounter. It becomes crystal clear.

6. The first time that you do this out-of-body meditation, keep in mind that you are witnessing a real person in a real setting. However, you are a witness without form, in a consciousness body. You will ordinarily not be seen. You have no arms, legs, eyes, ears, or nose. Your physical senses are replaced with conscious awareness.

7. Now look deeply into your loved one to determine what might be wrong in terms of overall health. You can see a lot with your new eyes. You can look deeply into the physical health of your subject, but also look to see if the health problem resides on emotional, mental, or spiritual levels of their being.

8. If you have permission from your subject to offer healing assistance, you can do so at this time. You can project your loving thoughts to the place of concern. You can project healing energy to your loved one.

9. When you sense that you have accomplished your goal, gently return to your own physical body by simply thinking about it.

10. Slowly gather yourself back in your physical body and carefully get to your feet when you feel ready.

11. Remote healings can be quick. Everything about experiences in heightened consciousness can be quick. You can accomplish a tremendous amount with only a few clicks off the clock back in the physical realm where your sleeping body reclines. Forget about time. It doesn't exist as we know it. It is not a matter of time, but duration. Change takes as long as it takes to occur. And when you return, your physical body will feel as though it's had a long and refreshing rest.

Recapitulation

• Did you see your loved one in precise detail? If your friend didn't look exactly the same as the last time you met, that's proof positive that this visit was real and not just a memory of how things looked to you in the past.

- In a state of higher consciousness, we can sometimes look at a problem with precise vision. Remember that you are no longer gazing upside down at light reflected off objects, as in the physical world and normal eyesight, but looking squarely at things with fresh eyes.

- If you observed something that you think is significant with regard to your friend's health, you could report that to your friend to have a medical professional check it out. This is the role of the perfect observer or witness.

- In the case of your pet, you can take direct action by contacting a veterinarian to check out your observation.

- In your consciousness body, you see with clarity without the need to rationalize. When you observe the anomaly in your loved one, you project energy from your own consciousness. This is like a healing thought-form that is projected point-blank, at close range. This will be more or less instinctive for your spirit. You are healing spirit to spirit. Think of this as a jump start from one healthy car battery to a car battery that is weakened.

- You might find yourself instinctively sending colored light as healing energy. Do not analyze the color that you send. You will know the right color by what you observe. You will sense what is needed and act spontaneously. The colors of healing energy that you project and transfer will likely correspond to the area that is ailing. You cannot make a bad determination or bad choice of healing energy during such a spirit-to-spirit healing visit.

- When we reach out to a friend with healing energy, this is a projection of our thoughts or consciousness. You cannot hurt your friend in this way or give him or her the wrong energy. You are connecting on a spirit-to-spirit level and cannot make a mistake. The energy that you project will be helpful in assisting your friend in healing, no matter how you project it or where you project it. All healing energy is beneficial. The body absorbs healing energy readily no matter how it is received.

LEAVING YOUR BODY FOR SHAMANIC SOUL RETRIEVAL

What You Need
- A quiet, isolated room where you can safely and comfortably recline in deep meditation.

- A mat, pad, blanket, or towel on which you can recline on your back.
- Comfortable, loose-fitting clothes, with your shoes removed.

Procedure

1. Reclining on your back with arms and feet slightly outstretched, close your eyes and visualize leaving your physical body when you reach higher consciousness to visit people and situations where you sense that you have lost parts of your essential life force, leaving you fragmented. Form pictures of these people and places and then tuck these pictures carefully in the back of your mind to retrieve when you reach a state of higher consciousness.

2. Now visualize leaving your physical body and visiting these people and places when you reach higher consciousness by retrieving the pictures you have formed in your mind's eye.

3. Tune out all external distractions and internal dialogue to put yourself in a state of deep meditation. Begin deep, controlled breathing.

4. You should leave your body to retrieve your lost fragments as soon as you put your physical body to sleep and reach a deep meditative state.

5. When you return to your physical body, you might consider whether there are any other places that you would like to visit for soul retrieval and repeat the process.

GOING BACK IN TIME FOR SELF-HEALING

What You Need

- A quiet, isolated room where you can safely and comfortably recline in deep meditation.
- A mat, pad, blanket, or towel on which you can recline on your back.
- Comfortable, loose-fitting clothes, with your shoes removed.

Procedure

1. Reclining in a meditative pose on your back with arms and legs extended, visualize leaving your body and going back to a time when you would like to heal yourself with energy. This could be a pivotal time in your past

when you first encountered an illness that has advanced throughout your life.

2. Form a picture in your mind's eye of this time and place with yourself at a younger age in the picture. Now tuck this picture in the back of your mind with the intent to bring it forward when you reach higher consciousness.

3. Tune out all external distractions and internal dialogue and reach a state of higher consciousness. Begin deep, controlled breathing. You will see a blank slate in your mind's eye and then automatically bring forward the picture you have visualized with the active intent to visit.

4. You will go immediately to this time and place in your past and send healing energy to yourself. This will happen pretty automatically as spirit takes control and you function in a state of higher awareness.

5. When you have returned to your physical body, slowly adjust to sensations returning to your body and take caution in opening your eyes and rising to your feet, as this will be a deep meditation that can be a bit disorienting.

GOING BACK IN TIME TO ASSIST SOMEONE

What You Need

- A quiet, isolated room where you can safely and comfortably recline in deep meditation.
- A mat, pad, blanket, or towel on which you can recline on your back.
- Comfortable, loose-fitting clothes, with your shoes removed.

Procedure

1. Use the same procedure as the above exercise for self-healing, except that you instead visualize a loved one that you intend to visit in the past for energy healing.

2. Keep in mind in your visualization that you are traveling outside your physical body and escaping the limitations of time and space to a state of pure conscious energy where real change and healing is easier than we experience in the gross, mundane world. As you go backward in time

and visit a scene you have recalled from the past, you travel at the speed of light.

GOING FORWARD IN TIME TO ASSIST OURSELVES

What You Need

- A quiet, isolated room where you can safely and comfortably recline in deep meditation.
- A mat, pad, blanket, or towel on which you can recline on your back.
- Comfortable, loose-fitting clothes, with your shoes removed.

Procedure

1. Reclining in a meditative pose on your back with arms and legs extended, visualize leaving your body and visiting a specific scene you create in your mind's eye of yourself in the future. In this scene, you are healing or assisting yourself in a way that will be helpful to you. It is not necessary to visualize exactly how you will assist yourself to effect change, but that you have a sense of what problems you might later encounter. It might be difficult to make the scene detailed, but try to form the scene as precisely as you can with yourself at a later age.

2. Tuck that picture in the back of your conscious mind with the active intent to bring it forward as a road guide at the moment you reach higher consciousness and stare into blankness.

3. Now tune out all external distractions and internal dialogue to put the physical body to rest and reach a state of higher consciousness in deep, deep meditation. Begin deep, controlled breathing.

4. Once you reach higher consciousness and stare at a blank slate in your mind's eye, your composed picture of where you intend to go and what to do should pop immediately into your mind's eye to take you forward in time.

5. You will be looking at a future version of yourself from a consciousness body that is invisible and not interactive with any person or situation in the future. Your spirit will sense what to do instinctively with its higher awareness and send pure energy to assist your future self to heal or effect

other changes that would otherwise be difficult in the physical realm.

6. When you return automatically to your physical body, take your time readjusting to physical sensations and slowly open your eyes and stand up. This is a deep meditation and can be disorienting.

Recapitulation

*   You have effortlessly left your physical body and the limitations of the manifest world of time and space to visit the past and the future. According to leading physicists, traveling to the past or the future involves traveling at the speed of light. Thus your higher consciousness as pure energy outside your physical body traveled faster than the speed of light.

*   You have conquered time travel, and you have done it without mirrors or particle separation facilities that smashed atoms to create big bang energy. Obviously, you are more than physical matter that reflects light as it strikes you at a specific instant. You are a light being encased in a physical body that you can leave now and then to travel as pure energy forward and backward in time wherever you desire to go. You are a time traveler.

7

Seventh Secret of Time

THE PRIMAL POWER OF
THE SEVEN RAYS

In order to fully appreciate time, perhaps we should look at a bigger picture. If we begin to think of time as the periodic waves of energy that descend on us as rays of light, then time as light energy seems to be coming to us through a refractor, prism, or filter that bends light into different colors of energy with various properties.

Before light reaches our physical world, it is bent or refracted by various celestial objects. The prismatic effect of bending light forms a spectrum of various light waves or frequencies that we perceive most commonly as different colors of light. We see only seven basic colors of light, and this shapes our worldview. The seven colors have various properties that affect people in different ways. Mystics have long studied these effects, and now modern psychologists also find this to be interesting and revealing. Perhaps the seven rays are the primal forces that shape our creation with varied opportunities, and we simply confuse this as time as it strikes us here and there in different ways.

For many years we had only the observations claimed by clair-voyants of the faint coloration of light energy that is part of the aura or energy body around life forces, including the human body. Their descriptions, consistent through the ages, have been of light energy seen as seven distinct colors, from red at one end of the visual spectrum to violet at the other end.

This visual spectrum was first attributed to observations by the ancient Greek scientist and philosopher Pythagoras. Beginning with the work of Sir Isaac Newton, scientists gained the ability to mea-sure the various frequencies or wavelengths of different colors. After Newton, Thomas Young was credited with an accurate measurement of the wavelengths of different colors of light in 1802. Today, scien-tists can measure the wavelengths of colors by how many light waves reach the eye in one second.

It might be interesting and revealing to note that the seven colors of the visible light spectrum—red, orange, yellow, green, blue, indigo, and violet—correspond to the seven notes of the diatonic musical scale. In ancient India, mystics have long observed the human body to have seven basic energy centers or chakras that correspond to these same seven col-ors, from red at the spine to violet at the crown of the head.

THE SEVEN COLORS OF THE CHAKRAS

In ancient Hindu tradition, the seven colors of light relate to the seven chakras that operate within the human body on a physical level and on all subtle energy body levels as well. This is, after all, the primal energy that empowers life, not only in humans but in other animals and other living organisms as well. We are self-regenerative dynamos who absorb, process, and transform the electromagnetic energy that is all around us and within us. When we do so normally, we are healthy.

The seven colors of light in the spectrum each relate to a specific area and function in the body. Red relates to the first (root) chakra, located at the base of the spine. Orange relates to the second chakra, located at the abdominal area. Yellow relates to the third chakra, located at the solar plexus. Green relates to the fourth chakra, located in the heart region. Blue relates to the fifth chakra, located in the throat area. Indigo relates to the sixth chakra, located at the forehead. Violet relates to the seventh (crown) chakra, located above the head. Clairvoyants are able to perceive this energy and have long been in agreement on the colors that they see at various energy points or chakras in the body. Kirlian cameras have also verified these colors associated with various parts of the body.

POWERS OF THE SEVEN LIGHT COLORS

There is primordial power in every experienced color of light, and every color has a distinctive signature and impact on life. In yogic healing, the long-held belief is that the color that is related to each specific chakra and the area of the body that it governs energizes us on physical and subtle body levels. The various properties of colors in the spectrum also have been shown to be useful in treating various areas of the body. Red is often used in color therapy to treat reproductive organs, urinary tracts, the rectal area, and red blood cells. Orange is used to treat the thyroid, kidneys, spleen, and colon. Yellow is used to treat the digestive system, liver, stomach, and lymph system. Green is used to treat the heart, lungs, and thymus. Blue is used to treat the larynx, thyroid, jaws, tonsils, mouth, and speech problems. Indigo is used to treat the eyes, brow-area headaches, hormonal imbalances, and developmental disorders. Violet is used to treat headaches, depression, balance problems, mental deficiency, nerves, and cancer.

Classically, metaphysical values have been assigned to the seven colors. Red relates to sex, vigor, and strength. Orange relates to stimulation, attraction, happiness, and kindness. Yellow relates to confidence, comfort, intense thought, and persuasion. Green relates to growth, wellness, fertility, finance, and energy. Blue relates to devotion, understanding, truth, sincerity, and serenity. Indigo relates to transformation, ambition, depression, and psychic matters. Violet relates to power, piety, sadness, and melancholy.

Clairvoyants who can see auras and the energy associated with the seven chakras often describe the spectrum of seven colors as faint or even pastel, but becoming bolder as the chakras actively process and transform energy throughout the body.

THE SEVEN RAYS

Helena Petrovna Blavatsky, author of *The Secret Doctrine,* introduced Westerners to the seven rays as divine lights that bend upon entering earth's atmosphere, creating a spectrum of color. These lights of various wavelengths, frequencies, and colors descend lovingly and unceasingly to earth, energizing everything they touch. In volume one of *The Secret Doctrine,* she said that the colored gemstones the gnostics used for healing represented the seven large stars of the Egyptian Great Bear constellation, the seven elemental powers, and the seven Rishis (seers) in the Hindu tradition. She said that the seven rays of the Vedic sun deity Vishnu represent the same concept as the astral fluid of the Kabbalists and that the seven emanations of the lower seven sephiroth* are actually the primary seven rays that can be found in every religion.

In volume two of *The Secret Doctrine,* Blavatsky examines the seven nervous plexuses of the body and the seven rays they radiate, noting that this principle is found in the *Rig Veda,* the mythology of Ahura Mazda, and the beliefs of the Incas and the Chinese Tao. She also remarks that the Egyptian god Osiris takes seven rays with him when he enters the solar boat.

In volume three of *The Secret Doctrine,* Blavatsky further describes the seven primeval rays as a group of celestial beings, gods, angels, Dyan

---

*In mystical Judaism, the Kabbalah describes ten powerful emanations, or sephiroth, which the Creator used to become manifest. Each of these spheres outlined on the Tree of Life for personal spiritual pathworking represents one of the ten stages of emanation and helps the student better understand creation.

Chohans, or powers. She said that this symbolism was later adopted by
Christianity as the Seven Angels of the Presence.

She saw the seven rays as seven primary forces in nature and in people or, according to the ancient Hindu viewpoint, the seven manifestations of God. In Blavatsky's Theosophy, the seven rays are said to be the
seven major types of light substances (spirit or wave/particle) that form
the created universe. They are also believed to convey divine qualities.

In the writings of two later Theosophists, Ernest Wood and
Geoffrey Hodson, each of the seven rays is associated with a different
kind of occult energy and a different color. This belief is now popular in the West and in energy healing. The seven-ray concept appears
in the modern New Age consciousness movement. The energy healing system of Reiki, for instance, requires a student to pass through a
sequence of levels by mastering the key to each level. The key for the
second level in Reiki training is the key of oneness, which is attained
by passing through each of the seven rays. In esoteric astrology today,
the seven rays are split into groups. The first two rays represent will
and wisdom, and the remaining five rays together form a group that
represents activity.

DEEPLY ROOTED IN MANY TRADITIONS

The concept of the seven rays as primal energy dates back as far as two
millenniums and is prevalent in many cultures of both the East and the
West. It was prevalent in mystery traditions that include the Christian
gnostics and the Roman Mithraic mysteries. From the sixth century
BCE seven rays were prevalent in the gnosticism of the Mediterranean
and the Middle Eastern region of Babylonia.

In 1894 Harvard historian S. F. Dunlap wrote that the idea of
Spirit as the ultimate cause is present in all of the great religions of the
East and that this idea can be found in the seven rays of the Chaldean
Mithra (the Sun God of the early inhabitants of ancient Babylonia) and
the seven days of Genesis. "The Chaldean Mithra had his seven rays;

and Moses had his seven days," he wrote. "The other planets which circling round the sun lead the dance as round the King of heaven receive from him with the light also their powers, while as the light comes to them from the sun so from him they receive their power that he pours out into the Seven Spheres of the Seven Planets of which the sun is the centre." Prior to the Christian era, this deity was known as the Io (the first form) or Sabaoth (the sun) and later described as Christos of the Resurrection of Souls. In the fourth century CE, Emperor Julian Saturnalia composed a "Hymn to the Solemn Sun" and spoke of unspeakable mysteries and the god of the seven rays, disguised as Julian the Chaldean.

In ancient Greek mythology, Zeus takes the bull form known as Taurus in order to win Europa's favor. Taurus is also associated with Aphrodite and other goddesses, as well as Pan and Dionysus. The face of Taurus, curiously, was said to gleam with seven rays of light.

The seven rays can even be found in texts and iconic art of the Catholic Church as early as the Byzantine era. In early Christian iconography, the dove of the Holy Ghost is shown with the emanation of seven rays, as is the image of the Madonna, often with doves. The Monastery of St. Catherine on Mount Sinai shows the transfiguration of Christ with seven rays of light shining from his luminous body. The Byzantine-style Saint Louis Cathedral in the United States features an engraved circle at the heart of the sanctuary with many symbols of the Holy Trinity and the curious inscription "radiating from this symbols are seven rays of light representing the seven gifts of the Holy Ghost."

The *Annunciation,* an oil painting by early Dutch master Jan van Eyck (1435), shows the annunciation by the Archangel Gabriel to the Virgin Mary that she will bear the son of God (Luke 1:26–38). In a prominent element of the complete work, the seven gifts of the Holy Spirit descend to her on seven rays of light from the upper window to the left, with the dove symbolizing the Holy Spirit following the same path.

Similarly, members of the Italian secret society called Knights of the Apocalypse in the late 1600s wore a star with seven rays on their breastplates. They fought to defend the Catholic Church against the Antichrist.

We also see the seven rays prominently in Hindu religious philosophy and scripture from ancient India. In the Gayatri prayer from the Vedas, the seven rays are described as emanations of the sun, identified with the creator of life. "The being who shines with seven rays, assuming the form of time and illuminates all," it reads, "naturally shines with seven rays . . . called light or effulgent power, the light of the Generator or Sun. . . . The light is the Sun; the Sun is the light. They are identical." The *Vishnu Purana,* a post-Vedic scripture, describes Vishnu entering "into the seven solar rays" and the "seven suns which the seven solar rays dilate at the consummation of all things."

Egyptologist Gerald Massey in 1881 described connections between Vedic scripture, ancient Egyptian mythology, and the gospel stories, noting the unity of the seven souls of the pharaoh, the seven arms of the Hindu god Agni, the seven stars in the hand of the Christ in the Book of Revelation, and the seven rays of the Chaldean god Iao on the healing gemstones of the gnostics. He also theorized that the "seven-rayed sun god of the Gnostic stones was also the Serpent Chenubis and the Second Beast in the Book of Revelation."

Art historian Ananda Coomaraswamy, curator of Asiatic art at the Museum of Fine Arts, Boston, wrote that the seven rays of the sun appear in both Hindu and Christian symbolism, representing similar concepts. In particular, he noted the symbolism of the seventh ray, which corresponds to the distinction between transcendent and immanent, infinite and finite. "The seventh ray alone," he wrote, "passes through the Sun to the super-solar Brahma worlds, where no sun shines—all that is under the sun being in the power of Death and all beyond Immortal."

THE SEVEN RAYS IN PEOPLE

New Zealand clairvoyant, author, and priest Geoffrey Hodson extended the efforts of earlier Theosophists such as H. P. Blavatsky, Ernest

Wood, and Charles W. Leadbeater to show how the seven rays as primeval, divine powers influence human life. In *The Call to the Heights* he showed how each person is born under the influence of one of the seven rays and is influenced by the unique properties of that particular ray in terms of personal strengths, basic attributes, and direction. It is interesting that Hodson's correspondences with regard to the seven rays are consistent with many earlier and later outlines of the influence of their primeval forces on the personal identity. Other lists of seven-ray correspondences might vary a little.

Note that Hodson found those born under the sign of Leo to be associated with the synthesis and source of all in regard to the seven rays. They tend to have clairvoyance and intuition and an affinity for all arts. Associated with the color orange, they are sun worshippers by nature. They gravitate toward pranic and magnetic healing. Their very symbol is the seven rays, depicted as a seven-pointed star with a dot in the center.

First-Ray People

The first ray, according to Hodson, ushers in and empowers leaders who are clairaudient with an acute sense of smell and a strong will. They are kingly, decisive, heroic, and dominant. They exhibit rulership in every activity they enter. Their strong willpower is expressed through the mind, emotions, and body. They have a determination to carry out decisions despite resistance. They are decisive and forceful with their eyes on a goal. Their sun sign is most likely Cancer or Aquarius, and their corresponding color is violet.

Second-Ray People

Second-ray people in Hodson's view are wise teachers and philanthropists who are driven by universal love. They have intuitive perception of a divine plan, are affectionate, share in the lives of others, and are helpful—even sacrificing their own interests and wishes. They are compassionate and filled with love and tenderness that is expressed physically and in heartfelt feelings. They exhibit deep concern for the suffering of others and spirituality in self-sacrificing acts. Their sun sign at birth is usually Gemini, Virgo, or Pisces, and their corresponding color is yellow.

Third-Ray People

Hodson saw third-ray people as philosophers who are driven by the power of thought with an increasing ability to comprehend underlying principles and understand nature's laws and procedures from many possible points of view. They are impartial administrators and directors who see logic and reason as the ultimate court of appeal and find a just solution to problems. They are not swayed by self-interest or personal desire. Their corresponding sun sign at birth is usually Libra or Taurus, and their corresponding color is indigo.

Fourth-Ray People

Fourth-ray people, Hodson said, are artistic people who are perceptive, meditative, and portray beauty. They have the ability to be inspired, moved, or influenced. They perform from the eternal and fundamental levels on one hand and the changing world on the other hand. They experience harmony and also demand it on personal and impersonal levels. They desire harmony between the inner and outer sides of life, between self and others, and between self and surroundings. They are known for charm and allure and are generally Sagittarius in terms of their sun sign at birth. Their corresponding color is generally blue.

Fifth-Ray People

Hodson depicts people who are energized and ushered into life by the fifth ray as scientists who are driven by logic, mental keenness, and accuracy. They passionately aspire to discover the true facts and how they apply. This interest goes beyond curiosity or just wanting to find quick answers to determining truth for truth's own sake, with both concrete and abstract truth sought and perhaps even worshipped as divine. They search below the surface for the ultimate truth. This begins with an instinctive and later conscious dissatisfaction with ignorance. Their sun sign at birth is generally Capricorn, and their corresponding color is usually green.

Sixth-Ray People

People driven by the energy of the sixth ray, according to Hodson, tend to be devotees and martyrs, characterized by devout loyalty and sacrificial love. They are often completely dedicated to a cause and totally selfless in pursuing what they perceive as the spiritual ideal and its expression. They are trustworthy and completely loyal with regard to their ideals and associations. They are single-minded in their pursuit of conscious self-identification with the supreme God. Their sun sign at birth tends to be Scorpio or Aries, and their corresponding color is red.

Seventh-Ray People

People who are driven by the energy of the seventh ray, in Hodson's book, are characterized by willpower, intellectual concepts, idealism, and appropriate action. With driving enthusiasm, such people eventually acquire concentrated thought, formed by will. In the awakened individual, this could lift a seventh-ray person to solar and cosmic levels of consciousness. These solar energies and awareness can eventually become their source and collaborators. The advanced seventh-ray person can see how the cosmos is actually a single whole. Seventh-ray persons are instinctively moved toward orderliness in everything that they do. Consequently, they are ritualistic by nature. Their life becomes stately, dignified, and orderly through ceremony. They are generally born under the sun sign of Cancer or Aquarius, and, like the first-ray people, their corresponding color is violet.

Determining Your Own Color

It's long been considered difficult to match human temperaments with
rays by color. One way to determine your own ray might be to review
the lists of personal characteristics given here and see which seem to
best define who you are and your drive in life. Personally speaking, as a
Gemini, I see my rays as a blending of colors, with the yellow of the second ray naturally predominant. The colors of the seven rays do blend as
they are absorbed by us and other life forms. Clairvoyants who describe
the colors around the chakras as they process energy often describe
blended colors, with one color most prominent.

MAGICAL TATTWAS

Brightly colored Tattwa cards have long been used to induce deep meditations and out-of-body experiences in India. Focusing only on the colors, the mystic goes into deep meditation and leaves the body. These
special cards are brightly colored so that the light that bounces off
them is striking to behold. They are printed over many times to create
a vibrant, bouncy color that is electric. Each card is a different color,
corresponding to the seven colors of the spectrum and seven colors of
the chakras. The concept is that the energy of the vibrant, electric colors will transform you. One popular way to use the magical Tattwas is
to meditate on each of the colors in turn as you work your way through
the various cards. Every one of the seven rays has special power to energize and transform you.

SOUND ENERGY

Another form of primeval energy that energizes us and our world on
all levels is sound energy. In measuring sound energy, the frequency is
determined by how many sound waves are made in one second. That
determines the note. That is similar to measuring light, where color is
determined by the number of light waves that reach the eye in one second.

We can associate specific notes of sound energy with specific colors of light energy. Here is a corresponding chart:

1.	Middle C	=	Red
2.	D	=	Orange
3.	E	=	Yellow
4.	F	=	Green
5.	G	=	Blue
6.	A	=	Indigo
7.	B	=	Violet

A master, perhaps, could arrange the notes in a beautiful harmony that triggers the music of life or music of creation. The right balance of sounds can restore and sustain our health and body energy as a self-regenerative system. In Native American folklore, there is the oral history of how the world was sung into creation. "In the beginning was the word," according to the Christian history of creation.

Perhaps this is what Pythagoras, the ancient Greek mathematician, philosopher, and astronomer, meant when he envisioned the *music of the spheres.* The founder of the Pythagorean mystery school saw a harmonic connection between movements of the celestial bodies and their numerical proportions. The balanced relationship between the sun, moon, and planets—so the theory goes—creates ratios of pure musical intervals and musical harmony. This music is not audible in a physical sense that we can hear with our ears, but as more of a harmonic concept with mathematical and spiritual overtones.

The early theory has traveled and found new roots in many other cultures throughout history. Some Indian yogis of the Surat Shabda Yoga tradition have described something similar to the music of the spheres in what they call *"the audible life stream."* Esoteric Christianity sometimes refers to something very similar to the music of the spheres in a state of consciousness they call "Second Heaven." Rosicrucian Max

Heindel describes the music of the spheres as being audible as an ocean of harmony in a lower region he called the "region of concrete thought." The harmonic music rolls over us, whether we perceive it or not.

WAVE PATTERN AND HARMONIC RESONANCE

Wave patterns can be measured in terms of sound energy waves or light energy waves, in much the same way as we analyze the complementary or disruptive patterns of water waves. Harmonic resonance, or matched frequencies of wave patterns, can establish health and well-being.

Research by scientist and medical doctor Andrija Puharich in experiments with psychic Uri Geller suggests that the frequency of thought-forms varies according to the application and that a harmonic frequency of the energy wave created by human consciousness could match the harmonic frequency of the earth. Dr. Puharich speculated that the instinctive kisses and healing thoughts of a mother for her baby project energy waves similar to the wave pattern found in all healthy life-forms. A harmonic frequency that matches the resonance of the earth and the natural healthy state of living beings would restore health to an injured or ill subject, Dr. Puharich said. To test this the doctor had Geller send healing thought-forms as energy to a glass of water for another person to drink, in an experiment similar to that of Mesmer in magnetizing a tub of water with his hands. The effects on the water and the subject were measurable.

We also can approach harmonic resonance by realizing the frequency of electromagnetic radiation as it strikes us and energizes us. Every day is slightly different, as the properties of the rays that fall lovingly and unceasingly on us vary in frequency, wavelength, and properties. Our subtle bodies as aspects of our spirit instinctively feel the difference and can adjust to the opportunities of the moment if we step outside our analytical lower mind long enough for higher consciousness to function for us. We can adjust our actions to the opportunities that are afforded by the new energy each day.

Like all living beings, we have within us the capacity to absorb the electromagnetic energy around us to become our personal energy. The trick might be in recognizing what kind of energy is immediately available for our imminent tasks. Maybe we should compile our "To Do Lists" and day planners with a little leeway, not slavishly charted in advance within fifteen-minute increments. The energy we need will come to us for everything on our little agendas, but not necessarily in the order that we have preordained.

Personally speaking, I know that some days I find no energy for the tasks that I have planned for that morning when I step outdoors into the rays of light. If I review the projects that I have planned for later in the day or perhaps for the next day, however, I can find a perfect match of energy. This, too, is harmonic resonance. By contrast, trying to fit new waves of energy (my energy) that are out of synch with the waves of energy streaming down from the heavens is like playing a blank note that is lost amid the other sounds.

It's easy to see how the quality of natural light changes dramatically throughout the year. Anyone who has seriously studied the art of photography or landscape painting recognizes that the quality of light varies from day to day and instant to instant. Professional landscapers and naturalists often keep journal entries of the quality of light at various times of the day in various locations. In North America, where I have worked as a photographer, I came to recognize that our light is generally delicate in color and brightness in the morning and very intense and dark in the late afternoon. In the Caribbean, the setting sun will often have an exotic dark orange or purple color. Photographers come to realize that not all light is white and that even blue light, as we are able to perceive it, has six known shades of blue.

HOW THE ANCIENTS LIVED IN THE LIGHT

The ancients realized the changing quality of natural light and patterned their activities around it with an interactive wheel of the year. Their pagan ceremonies honored the changes of light throughout the year as it changed nature around them and their kinship with nature. They would welcome the spring by honoring the spring equinox with rites to acknowledge the pattern of renewal and rebirth. They would celebrate what we now call Groundhog Day or Valentine's Day around February 2 with a festival of lights to remember the sun that personified Solar Logos. This was a happy time of growing warmth. Springtime was a time to bless and plant seeds in a full moon after the spring equinox. The early pagans would dance around a May pole around the first of May and wash their faces in the first dew of May to ensure the fertility of the earth.

They would celebrate summer solstice with a midsummer festival to honor the Sun God who had reached his greatest glory and coupled with the Earth Goddess. Toward the end of July or first of August, they would celebrate the bounty of the earth with a feast of bread. In the third week of September, during autumn equinox, they would say goodbye to the Sun God in decline and the Earth Mother retiring to rest through the winter. It was a time to give thanks for the blessings of the earth's many gifts of abundance and prepare for the rest cycle in nature when the new seeds rest deep in the earth and trees prepare for brief slumber and shed their summer leaves.

They would celebrate at the end of October with a special night when the world of spirit and the physical world are closest and the veil that separates the worlds is at its thinnest. All Hallows Eve or Halloween was also traditionally celebrated by a feast of the dead where foods such as apples were left on doorsteps. This special time was also used to reflect on the fabric of life and changes all around us as nature prepares for a new cycle of growth.

The ancients celebrated winter solstice, in what has become Christmas time or Yule for many, to note a time of least sunlight when the Sun God is preparing his return. It was a time to celebrate the coming of light out of the darkness and an ideal time to gather with friends to celebrate around a fire, burning log, or illuminated tree to remember the gifts of nature.

Folk or pagan ceremonies also recognized the different properties of the reflected light of the moon throughout the year in terms of new moon, waxing moon, full moon, and waning moon. The new moon each month is the ideal time for endings and beginnings. The second phase of the moon, the waxing moon, relates to development, growth, and projects that are nearing completion. The third quarter or full moon is a time for fulfillment and the ideal time for love, magic of the heart, health, success, and giving thanks. It is also associated with maturity and the culmination of plans. The ancients regarded the fourth phase or waning moon as a time for retreat, reflection, reorganization, and reconstruction. It was also associated with disintegration and planning for the new moon.

The ancients, who lived closer to nature, also recognized the different properties of the moon each month. The January moon was called the Wolf Moon or Ice Moon. It is typically purple in color, a reminder of the myth of Persephone locked in the underworld, symbolic of the passing phase of land imprisoned beneath a sheet of ice. The February moon was the Blue Storm Moon, associated with water. Rains and raging bodies of water promised to restore spring to the land, which had been locked in an icy deadlock. The ancients felt a confidence in February that waters would flow again and the frozen grip of winter would be released on the land. They called the March moon the Chaste Moon. It represented Persephone's annual return from the underworld to life in the spring. This moon is white and brings freshness, cleanliness, and new beginnings. The April moon was called the Seed Moon. It is light green in color and ushers in the growing season when the land renews its green mantle. Seeds that have been sleeping in the earth begin stirring to life.

The moon in May was known as the Hare Moon. It was associated with fertility and the Goddess. It is pink in color, suggesting love and romance. As spring bursts into glory, the reproductive drives are energized by the new cycle. The June moon was called the Dyad or Pair Moon. Orange is the color of this moon. The ancients saw God in the bright sun and Mother Nature in the green fields in this moon. The

July moon was called the Mead Moon. It is yellow like honey in mead. The ancients celebrated the end of the growing season toward the end of July with evening song and dance by the light of this moon. The August moon was called the Wort Moon. It is green in color, the color of the rich, green earth that is heavy with harvest in August. The ancients celebrated in the light of this moon by honoring plant life and how it nourishes us. The September moon was the Barley Moon that rises before the autumn equinox. It mirrors the color of grain that is harvested at this time of year. The October moon was called the Blood Moon and is identified with the red blood of animals slaughtered at this time of year. The November moon was called the Snow Moon. It glows with a soft blue and silver color. The December moon was called the Oak Moon. It is a black moon, seen in the darkness of the short days in December.

MERGING WITH THE LIGHT

Living in harmony with the energy all around us might seem like a commonsense approach for living a balanced life in tune with the forces of nature. Strangely, however, most people seem to choose division over harmony, separateness over union, and conflict over cooperation. We do not blend, but seek to bend things to our individual desire of what we think we want right now. Nature just doesn't work that way. Every living thing absorbs, processes, and transforms electromagnetic radiation as a divine gift to energize and regenerate. The question remains, however, how we as analytical creatures choose to transform and project the universal energy around us as light strikes us at this exact instant in the Now. This is our moment. This is our time to act.

The Native American dream walker steps outside time and space to visit the grandfather of all, the unifying spirit of animals as guides and ancestors in an energy realm beyond individualism. The samadhi mystic in the East seeks to merge with the Oneness of All, as Blavatsky described the highest level of consciousness. As animals that live so far outside the harmony of the spirit realm, however, it is difficult for most of us to recognize how it is possible to escape the illusions of our physical world that we are alone, in conflict, and trapped in a three-dimensional world of matter. But our spirit longs to be free. Our consciousness as pure energy is perfectly capable of leaving our physical bodies to escape the limitations of fixed time and space. Once free, we find that meaningful healing and real change is possible in the unmanifest realm of pure energy. The exercises given here will help you to actualize your innate healing and harmonizing potentials.

READING SUBTLE BODY ENERGY COLORS

What You Need

- A quiet, private room.
- Loose-fitting, comfortable clothing, with shoes removed.
- Two straight-backed wooden chairs on which to sit.
- A second person who is willing to allow you to observe his or her subtle body and energy fields.

Procedure

1. Sit in a chair, facing your friend in the other chair. Both of you should have your feet firmly on the ground and your posture erect. Do not cross your hands or any part of your body, but rather let the energy within you flow freely.

2. Ask your friend to be still and quiet.

3. Visualize yourself seeing the natural colors of energy that surround your friend's physical body and successfully reading these light colors. Form a picture of yourself doing this activity and then tuck away this focused intent in the back of your consciousness to bring forward as soon as you enter higher consciousness.

4. Now tune out all external distractions of the physical world and your inner dialogue.

5. Begin deep, controlled breathing through your nostrils.

6. When you focus on a blank slate in your mind's eye, your visualized intent will spring forward automatically as a picture of what you have planned to do.

7. Turn your head toward your friend and allow your gaze to shift out of focus a little to the left to scan your friend's subtle energy body. Allow your higher awareness to interpret what it "sees" or senses in terms of energy colors. You will see a pale color. As you continue to focus your attention, you will begin to see the color more distinctly. Eventually, you will note the pattern of the energy field as well as the color. After you have observed a color in one area, move your gaze to another area of the body.

8. Gaze off the shoulders and focus your attention. Then move your gaze to the area around the head on both sides of the head and then above the head. Focus your attention until you have successfully scanned and read the color or colors in this region of the body.

9. Scan the area that surrounds the torso for subtle body energy colors. Do not analyze, but just allow yourself to carefully observe.

10 Scan the area off the legs for subtle body colors.

11. Now observe whether you can detect energy somewhat farther from the body, either high above the head or a distance from the sides of the body. Focusing your awareness, determine the colors and pattern of the energy fields.

12. When you have read the entire energy field of your friend, return to normal consciousness in your physical body.

Recapitulation

• As soon as you have finished your energy scanning and returned to normal consciousness, quickly itemize the energy fields that you have observed in terms of colors and patterns. Note where these energy patterns were formed in relation to your friend's body.

• Now is the time to analyze what you have observed, based on what you have learned with regard to subtle body energy and color properties.

• Note that this is not an easy exercise the first time; it requires patience to slowly "dial in" the energy colors and patterns of the subtle body. The colors will appear faint at first, and energy patterns might not be immediately obvious to you. This will require extremely focused awareness on your part. This exercise will only work if you have tuned out your physical sensations and normal brain functions and entered a state of heightened consciousness where higher awareness replaces sensory perception as a keener tool of observation.

THE KALEIDOSCOPE

What You Need

- A quiet, private room where you can meditate in peace.
- Loose-fitting, comfortable clothing, with shoes removed.
- A mat, pad, blanket, or folded towel on which to meditate on your back.
- Light from an unshielded window or else an interior light.

Procedure

1. Recline on your back with arms and legs slightly extended in the classic "dead man" yoga pose.

2. Close your eyes most of the way, but allow some light through your eyelashes.

3. Visualize the focused intent to actively and purposely absorb, process, and transform light internally when you reach a state of higher awareness in meditation. You will begin by transforming white light into yellow light and then yellow light into orange light. Then you will transform the orange light into red light. Finally, you will transform the red light into black, with the presence and potential of all lights blended together. Picture having done this successfully. Now tuck a picture of this process in the back of your consciousness to carry with you into higher consciousness.

4. Tune out all external distractions and internal dialogue and focus only on a blank screen in your mind's eye. Begin deep, controlled breathing through your nostrils.

5. When you reach a state of heightened consciousness, the intent that you have brought forward with you will allow you to focus immediately on color transformation.

6. The blank screen in your mind's eye is soon filled with white light, just as the light filters through your half-shut eyelashes. Focus intently on this

white light and consciously transform this white light into yellow light with the force of your will, projected from your abdomen.

7. The yellow that you initially see might be pale. As you focus on it, you will be able to transform it into a bolder, darker, and more energetic yellow.

8. When the yellow seems "bouncy" with electric energy, then begin to transform the yellow light into orange light. Focus your attention on the orange light; with your causal body and the force of your will, transform the pale orange light into a bolder, more energetic orange.

9. Transform the orange light into red light. Focus your attention on the red light to make it bolder and more energetic.

10. When the red becomes bouncy with energy, transform it into black with the presence and potential energy of all light blended into black.

11. When you have experienced the energy potential in the black, let it go.

12. Return to your physical body and take care in slowly opening your eyes and getting to your feet.

Recapitulation

- Do not be discouraged if it takes you a long while to transform the colors. You are actually transforming the energy level of the light energy that you have absorbed and processed within you. It is not an easy exercise, but something that you can certainly do with enough focused attention and practice. Change takes just as long as it takes. We cannot measure such transformation in terms of time that is required, but rather duration.

- The colors initially will appear to you as soft, almost pastel colors. This is much the way the aura and chakras appear as they routinely process energy. When the energy is charged up and ready to jump to another level of frequency, then it becomes bolder, darker, and bouncy with a buildup of intense energy.

- In a sense, you are manifesting these colors within you. More precisely, however, you are transforming electromagnetic energy that you have absorbed and processed. This personal ability to transform the colors of light energy demonstrates that you are a dynamo or generator that converts potential energy into active, electromagnetic energy.

MANIFESTING AND PROJECTING COLOR

Now that you have learned to transform electromagnetic energy, you should be able to manifest and project color with all of the energetic power of light in every frequency of the visible spectrum.

What You Need

- A quiet, private room where you can meditate in peace.
- Loose-fitting, comfortable clothing, with shoes removed.
- A mat, pad, blanket, or folded towel on which to meditate on your back.
- A friend who has agreed to let you send healing energy to him or her. (This might also be a pet.)

Procedure

1. Recline on your back with arms and legs extended.
2. Visualize a specific color of light that should assist your friend and prove healing. You can determine what color of light energy might be most helpful by either using your intuition or doing an astral scan to determine what chakra is not emitting the color of energy normally associated with it. In either case, remember that any color of light you send can be absorbed and used as good healing energy. There are no bad choices. Tuck that picture of the light energy you want to transfer somewhere in the back of your consciousness to bring with you into deep meditation.
3. Tune out all external distractions and internal dialogue, focusing on a blank slate in your mind's eye. Begin deep, controlled breathing through your nostrils.
4. When you reach a state of higher consciousness, the picture of your focused intent should come forward automatically to fill the blank slate in your mind's eye.
5. Begin to transform the light within you into a specific color of energy. Slowly the color will begin to form on the slate in your mind's eye. Focus your attention on the color and with the power of your will intensify this color until it is bold and bouncy with energy.

6. When the color in your mind's eye has become fully energized, send it to your friend by simply thinking of your friend. To make certain that the energy was dispatched, think of sending the energy directly to your friend, encapsulated in a thought-form of your pure consciousness.

7. Like a magnet, your healing thought-form is drawn to your dear friend with the specific energy attached to it.

8. Once your awareness senses that the healing energy has been sent and received, you should return automatically to your normal, physical consciousness.

Recapitulation

• It is also possible to follow your thought-forms to your distant friend. By thinking about your friend and wanting to join him or her, you can be instantly there. As we have learned in the "Reading Subtle Body Energy Colors" exercise on page 147, you should be able to scan your friend's subtle body to observe the energy that you have projected being absorbed by your friend. See it mingling with the colors of energy in your friend's own energy fields.

• Later, you can thank your friend for the opportunity to help his or her natural self-regeneration.

Energy is universal and something to be shared. Energy comes to each one of us as opportunity of the moment, our special instant filled with the potential of Now. Radiant energy flows through us and energizes us naturally as light beings held earthbound only by our dense, physical encasements. Our conscious energy can escape the physical limitations of earthbound time and space. Outside these physical restrictions, the possibilities for change are limitless.

Bibliography

Albert, Richard (Ram Dass). *Be Here Now.* New York: Crown, 1971.

Arkani-Hamed, Nima, Savas Dimopoulous, and Georgi Dvali. "The Universe's Unseen Dimensions." *Scientific American,* August 2000.

Arntz, William, Betsy Chasse, and Mark Vicente. *What the Bleep Do We Know!?* DVD. Los Angeles, Calif.: 20th Century Fox, 2005.

Aurobindo, Sri. *The Secret of the Veda.* Pondicherry, India: Sri Aurobindo Ashram Publication, 1971.

Backster, Cleve. *Primary Perception: Biocommunication with Plants, Living Foods, and Human Cells.* Anza, Calif.: White Rose Millennium Press, 2003.

Bailey, Alice A. *The Seven Rays of Life: A Compilation.* New York: Lucis Publishing Co., 1995.

Barbour, Julian. *The End of Time: The Next Revolution in Physics.* New York: Oxford University Press, 2001.

Becker, Robert. "The Direct Current Control System." *New York State Journal of Medicine* 62 (April 15, 1962).

Bell, Madison Smartt. *Lavoisier in the Year One: The Birth of a New Science in an Age of Revolution.* New York: W. W. Norton & Co., 2006.

Besant, Annie. *Thought Power: Its Control and Culture.* Wheaton, Ill.: Quest Books, 1967.

Besant, Annie, and Charles W. Leadbeater. *Thought-Forms.* Adyar, India: Theosophical Publishing Society, 1901.

Blavatsky, Helena Petrovna. *The Secret Doctrine.* Adyar, India: Theosophical Publishing House, 1979.

———. *Two Books of the Stanzas of Dyzan.* Adyar, India: Theosophical Publishing House, 1986.

Bowman, Carol. *Children's Past Lives: How Past Life Memories Affect Your Child.* New York: Bantam, 1998.

Braschler, Von. *Chakra Reading & Color Healing.* Baltimore, Md.: PublishAmerica, 2005.

———. *Perfect Timing: Mastering Time Perception for Personal Excellence.* St. Paul, Minn.: Llewellyn Publications, 2002.

Braschler, Von, and Mari Coryell. *A Magical Journal: A Personal Journey through the Seasons.* Blaine, Wash.: Phoenix Publishing, 2003.

Castenada, Carlos. *Journey to Ixtlan.* New York: Washington Square Press, 1991.

———. *A Separate Reality.* New York: Pocket Books, 1991.

———. *Tales of Power.* New York: Pocket Books, 1991.

Coomaraswamy, Ananda K. *The Door in the Sky: Coomaraswamy on Myth and Meaning,* from originals in the Bollinger Series. Princeton, N.J.: Princeton University Press, 1940–1947 ed.

Crowley, Aleister. *Magick without Tears.* Las Vegas: New Falcon Publications, 1991.

Dossey, Larry. *Healing Words: The Power of Prayer and the Practice of Medicine.* New York: HarperCollins, 1993.

Emoto, Masaru. *The Hidden Messages in Water.* New York: Atria Books, 2005.

———. *The Miracle of Water.* New York: Atria Books/Beyond Words, 2007.

Fisher, Joey, and David Fisher. *Joey the Hitman: The Autobiography of a Mafia Killer.* Jackson, Tenn.: Da Capo Press, 2002.

Gott, J. Richard. *Time Travel in Einstein's Universe: The Physical Possibilities of Travel through Time.* New York: Mariner Books, 2002.

Heline, Corinne. *The Esoteric Music of Richard Wagner.* La Canada, Calif.: New Age Press, 1974.

Hodson, Geoffrey. *The Call to the Heights.* Wheaton, Ill.: Quest Books, 1975.

Jerome, John. *The Sweet Spot in Time.* New York: Touchstone, Simon & Schuster, Inc., 1980.

Karagulla, Shafica, and Dora Van Gelder Kunz. *The Chakras and the Human Energy Fields.* Wheaton, Ill.: Theosophical Publishing House, 1998.

Kilner, Walter. *The Human Aura*. New York: Citadel Press, 1965.

Krishnamurti, Jiddu. *Commentaries on Living*. Wheaton, Ill.: Theosophical Publishing House, 1995.

Leadbeater, C. W. *The Chakras*. Wheaton, Ill.: Theosophical Publishing House, 1997.

Massey, Gerald. *The Natural Genesis*. Baltimore, Md.: Black Classic Press, 1998.

McLuhan, Marshall, and Quentin Fiore. *The Medium Is the Message*. New York: Random House, 1967.

Merleau-Ponty, Maurice. *Phenomenology of Perception*. Translated by Colin Smith. London: Rutledge & Kegan, 1962.

Miller, Barbara Stoler, trans. *The Bhagavad-Gita*. New York: Quality Paperback Book Club, 1998.

Millman, Dan. *The Warrior Athlete*. Walpole, N.H.: Stillpoint Publishing, 1991. (Since republished as *The Inner Athlete*.)

Montgomery, S. R. *Second Law of Thermodynamics*. Oxford: Pergamon, 1966.

Nagy, Andras M. *The Secrets of Pythagoras*. Charleston, S.C.: CreateSpace, 2007.

Olcott, Henry Steele. *Old Diary Leaves*. Wheaton, Ill.: Quest Books, 1975.

Ostrander, Sheila, Lynn Shroeder, and Ivan T. Sanderson. *Psychic Discoveries behind the Iron Curtain*. New York: Bantam Books, 1971.

Ouspensky, P. D. *Tertium Organum*. Kila, Mont.: Kessinger Publishing Company, 1998.

Paulson, Genevive Lewis. *Energy Focused Meditation*. St. Paul, Minn.: Llewellyn Publications, 2000.

Pierrakos, John. *Core Energetics*. Mendocino, Calif.: Core Evolution Publishing, 2005.

Plato. *Complete Works by Plato*. Indianapolis, Ind.: Hackett Publishing Company, 1997.

Puharich, Andrija. *Uri: The Original and Authorized Biography of Uri Geller—The Man Who Baffled Scientists*. London: W. H. Allen, 1974.

Roberts, Jane. *The Oversoul Seven Trilogy*. San Raphael, Calif.: Amber-Allen Publishing, 1995.

Sakellarios, Stephen. *In Another Life: Reincarnation in America*. DVD. Myrtle Beach, S.C.: Gold Thread Video Productions, 2002.

Shroder, Tom. *Old Souls: Compelling Evidence from Children Who Remember Past Lives.* New York: Simon & Schuster, 2001.

Skolimowski, Henryk. *Theatre of the Mind.* Wheaton, Ill.: Quest Books, 1984.

Smith, Ingram. *Truth Is a Pathless Land: A Journey with Krishnamurti.* Wheaton, Ill.: Theosophical Publishing House, 1990.

Steiger, Brad. *One with the Light: Authentic Near-Death Experiences that Changed Lives and Revealed the Beyond.* New York: Signet, 1994.

———. *Words from the Source.* Englewood Cliffs, N.J.: Prentice-Hall, Inc., 1975.

Stevenson, Ian. *Children Who Remember Previous Lives.* Jefferson, N.C.: McFarland, 2000.

———. *Twenty Cases Suggestive of Reincarnation: Second Edition, Revised and Enlarged.* Charlottesville: University of Virginia Press, 1980.

Stone, Robert B. *The Secret Life of Your Cells.* West Chester, Pa.: Whitford Press, 1994.

Tiller, William A., Walter Dibble, and Michael Kohane. *Conscious Acts of Creation.* Walnut Creek, Calif.: Pavior Publishing, 2001.

Tolle, Eckert. *The Power of Now: A Guide to Spiritual Enlightenment.* Novato, Calif.: New World Library, 2004.

Tompkins, Peter, and Christopher Bird. *The Secret Life of Plants.* New York: Avon, 1974.

Twitchell, Paul. *The Tiger's Fang.* Menlo Park, Calif.: Illuminated Way Press, 1967.

Watts, Alan. *The Way of Zen.* New York: Pantheon, 1974.

Wells, H. G. *The Time Machine.* New York: Simon & Schuster, 2004.

Wood, Ernest. *The Seven Rays.* Wheaton, Ill.: Quest Books, 1976.

Index

BOOKS OF RELATED INTEREST

Shamanism for the Age of Science
Awakening the Energy Body
by Kenneth Smith

The Subtle Energy Body
The Complete Guide
by Maureen Lockhart, Ph.D.

Shamanic Breathwork
Journeying beyond the Limits of the Self
by Linda Star Wolf

Transcending the Speed of Light
Consciousness, Quantum Physics, and the Fifth Dimension
by Marc Seifer, Ph.D.

Chakras
Energy Centers of Transformation
by Harish Johari

Microchakras
InnerTuning for Psychological Well-being
by Sri Shyamji Bhatnagar and David Isaacs, Ph.D.

The Akashic Experience
Science and the Cosmic Memory Field
by Ervin Laszlo

DMT: The Spirit Molecule
A Doctor's Revolutionary Research into the Biology of
Near-Death and Mystical Experiences
by Rick Strassman, M.D.

INNER TRADITIONS • BEAR & COMPANY
P.O. Box 388
Rochester, VT 05767
1-800-246-8648
www.InnerTraditions.com

Or contact your local bookseller